"Good elementary educators have always provided their students with some awareness of the world of work. Others have added innovations as the concern for career education has risen. More are willing but do not know how."

This book provides a foundation for all those teachers who understand the necessity of helping students become aware of the world of work. It approaches the task with three primary considerations in mind:

First, the early acquisition of those values often associated with work will make personal adjustment easier for the student

er
on
he
tary

her

Kenneth B. Hoyt
Nancy M. Pinson
Darryl Laramore
Garth L. Mangum

Olympus Publishing Company ⬤ Salt Lake City, Utah

ISBN 0-913420-05-0 (Cloth)
ISBN 0-913420-06-9 (Paper)

Library of Congress Catalog Card Number: 73-78952

Contents

Preface

Career Education: What It Is and How to Do It, by Hoyt, Evans, Mackin, and Mangum, is now in its fifth printing — which says something about the hunger for substantive "how to do it" information on career education. Given the past track record, three years of career education as the first priority of the U.S. Office of Education is also something of a phenomenon. But if career education is to spread throughout the educational system and be serviceable from "womb to tomb," detailed, practicable suggestions must be available for every stage of the preparation and pursuit of a successful working life.

The elementary school is the logical place to begin to provide such material. Hopefully, this book will be useful for both preservice and inservice teacher training, as an inspiration for elementary school administrators, and as a day-by-day guide for classroom teachers in elementary schools.

The book has profited from review and suggestions from Dr. Rupert N. Evans of the University of Illinois. Dr. Elwood Peterson and his staff at the Brigham Young University's Career Advisement Center supplied most of the material in chapter 5. Anyone interested in career development is of course indebted to Dr. Sidney P. Marland, Jr., now Assistant Secretary for Education in the U.S. Department of Health, Education and Welfare for his coining of the term "career education" and his persistent championship of the concepts.

This is the first of what we plan as a series of "how to do it" books on career education aimed at the home, the junior high, the high school, post-secondary education, and manpower programs. The authors may vary according to their expertise and interests, but they have in common a commitment to enhancing the satisfactions to be gained from working life. There is more to life than work, but there is little in a life that is not productive in service to others and in assurance of self-worth.

5

1

Career Education:
Basic Premises, Promises, and Problems

That career education — purely as a concept without definition, budget, or program to explain, motivate, or implement it — could attract such widespread interest and commitment since its advocacy in early 1971 by Assistant Secretary for Education Sidney P. Marland, Jr., is remarkable. Purchasing a commitment by way of major outflows of federal funds, if and only if guidelines are followed, is the common route to "education reform." New funds were intended as the carrot to attract allegiance to the career education concept. Yet failure of these funds to appear, though it understandably has slowed the advance, has not stopped the spread of the idea. Applications are few and rudimentary around the country, but are growing in all levels of the education system . . . elementary, secondary, and post-secondary.

As with every new major educational concept, one of the battle cries of its proponents is that career education must begin in the elementary school. Experienced elementary educators who have lived through other educational "revolutions" are sure to be skeptical. They have experienced too many other "reforms," coming to suspect that the reason educators say that action must begin in the elementary school is to provide those above this level with some excuse when the reforms fail. In view of the relatively great number of years expected to elapse for most stu-

7

dents between the elementary school and their entry into occupational society, this suspicion is almost certain to exist in the case of career education.

Further suspicion is sure to be aroused when persons, ignorant of elementary education, urge elementary educators to provide young students with their first awareness of the world of work. (After all, good elementary school teachers have been doing this for years!) Few major changes in elementary education are called for if this is all that career education asks of the elementary school.

However, both of these suspicions of career education are unfounded. There are basic and serious reasons for saying that if it is to attain its goals, career education *must begin in the elementary school.* There are equally serious reasons for asking for major directional changes in elementary education to be made in the name of career education. This chapter defends these two contentions, identifying the combination of societal and educational forces leading to the current career education emphasis and defining and discussing the basic nature of career education as an educational concept. It outlines briefly the major kinds of problems that career education faces as it struggles for meaningful integration into the total pattern of American education. Subsequent chapters carry the burden of describing "how to do it" in the elementary school.

Sources of the Career Education Movement

Education and work, two of our most basic historical values, are both in trouble in the United States. Education suffers largely because it has given insufficient attention to the role of work in the life-style and values of the individual; work suffers because educators and philosophers have failed in adapting traditional work values to the needs of a new and more complex age. Elementary educators, more than those involved in any other phase of the formal education process, are responsible for inculcating basic values and fundamental skills.

It is not surprising therefore to find that as career education has progressed from an advocacy to a movement, its most rapid advancement has been achieved at the elementary school level. In no other stage of the education system is the teacher and administrator more concerned with the whole of the child's development and preparation. Elsewhere, education is fragmented into subject matter areas. Only in elementary school is the student approached as whole and unique.

Good elementary educators have always provided their students with some awareness of the world of work. Others have added innovations as the concern for career education has risen. More are willing but do not know how. Why is career education needed . . . what is it . . . how can it be applied in the elementary school? These are vital questions for every classroom teacher, administrator, and parent concerned for the lifelong welfare of young human beings.

Social and Economic Impetus for Career Education

The case for career education must be made in the larger society. It is basically a societal crisis, not educational, that has created the call for career education. Society has never urged educational reform because noneducators became concerned for the welfare of the schools. Rather, all major educational reforms have grown from broader societal concerns that have led people to turn to the education community as part of the needed solution. The last major example of this phenomenon was the Elementary and Secondary Education Act of 1965, which grew out of the concerns of the war on poverty. Prior to that, the National Defense Education Act of 1958 emerged from concern with the Soviet ability to orbit a missile in space before the United States had attained that capability. It is no different in the case of career education. A variety of economic and social problems gave labor market manifestations, leading to demands for more effective preparation for working life.

Much of the societal concern motivating demands for career education is based, rightly or wrongly, on the assumption that the American society — and particularly its youth — is less work-oriented than in past generations. The most commonly quoted statistic is the doubling of numbers of public assistance recipients to fourteen million in only five years. Higher unemployment and lower labor force participation for youth are other symptoms often noted. Less attention is given to the millions who work full time/full year at grubby jobs which do not pay enough to raise them and their families out of poverty.

Disappointment with labor market performance is not limited to the poor and unemployed. Many with reasonably well-paid jobs find them less than satisfactory. A few young people and some older ones reject the working society and pursue other life-styles. Absenteeism in industry has risen in most industrial countries, and workers, particularly younger ones, dramatize their unrest with strikes over working conditions. Increasing specialization, once the *sine qua non* of mass production and industrialization, is giving way to job enrichment in some forward-looking companies here and abroad. While the American employment system continues to demonstrate the highest man-hour productivity in the world, the average annual rate of increase in that productivity is greater in several other nations.

Whether that continually rising productivity which sparked American industrial might and prosperity can continue its traditional pace is an issue of concern to economists, businessmen, and public policy makers at the highest levels. The transfer of labor and other resources from traditionally low-productivity agriculture to higher productivity manufacturing and transportation was a key factor in past productivity growth, as was increasing capitalization of agriculture. Improved health and education of workers and better management were important contributors, but a traditional American drive to succeed and excel in material ways provided motivational force. Transition from a goods-producing to a service- and information-producing economy cannot offer the same almost automatic productivity growth. With education and health services widespread, there are less productivity gains available from mere quantitative additions. The threat of environmental pollution adds the question of whether more and more and bigger and bigger are in fact better and better.

If motivation for economic success and occupational advancement also falters, can productivity growth — the only significant source of improvement in per capita national income — possibly keep living standards on an upward trend? Will even the continuance of the traditional upward trend of productivity be sufficient to meet the nation's domestic and international commitments; and if not, how can that rate of increase be accelerated?

This is not to suggest that failures of the education system can be blamed for these conditions. Nor do we suggest that those who suffer from unemployment and poverty are less committed to work as the preferred source of income than others. We merely note that advocates of education have promised to alleviate such problems. Policy makers and taxpayers have thought that they were buying solutions to these and other problems through the tremendous increases in the resources allocated to American education during the last generation, and both groups have been disappointed that the problems have not responded to the promised delivery.

All of the symptoms discussed above should be adequate evidence that all is not well in the American world of work. Viewing public education as a contributor to preparation for work opens no happier vistas.

Educational Forces behind Career Education

The call for career education stems in part from a general growing dissatisfaction with American education at all levels on the part of students, parents, and the general public. This dissatisfaction can be read into the large number of school bond issues that have failed in recent years, and in the increasing unwillingness of taxpayers to vote increased funds for educational purposes. More and more people are viewing our education system — from the elementary school through the graduate college — as irrelevant and unresponsive to current societal demands.

The fifth report of the National Advisory Council on Vocational Education recognized the condition in these words:

> There is an educational consumer revolt developing in our land today. . . . Public officials responsible for education, both elected and appointed, need to be reminded of Alexander Hamilton's statement, "Here, Sir, the people govern. . . ."

The several bases for this general dissatisfaction are easily specified. Each can be described in ways that hold implications for change in the elementary school. One basis for criticism is the growing recognition that 80 percent of secondary school students are preparing to do what 80 percent in fact will *not* do; that is, graduate from college. Approximately eight in ten of today's secondary education students are enrolled in either the college preparatory or the general education curriculum that allows people to be prepared for work only after college attendance. Yet three out of four of those who begin high school complete it, one-half of those who do so go on to college, and one-half of those who enter college graduate.

The enrollment ratio between academic and occupational education in the high school reflects the societal myth that worships the college degree as the best and surest route to career success. Certainly there are reasons other than occupational for seeking a college education, and there are numerous occupations for which college training is required or appropriate. Yet all elementary education teachers who discuss parental aspirations in the course of parent-teacher conferences discover the career myth underlying reasons for seeking education for their children. Far too often, the myth is reinforced by the elementary school teacher who *is* a college graduate. This reinforcement occurs in conferences held with parents and in the curriculum content presented daily to the elementary school students which emphasizes the contributions of the college trained and assumes that "all good children will go there someday."

Of every hundred students entering the first grade, only fourteen ever attain a baccalaureate degree. This statistic has been ignored long enough. Fortunately, students have been wiser than their parents, teachers, and school administrators. The U.S. Department of Labor predicts that less than 20 percent of all jobs in the 1970–80 period will require a baccalaureate degree. It is undoubtedly more than coincidence that this is approximately the same proportion as the percentage of beginning high school students who, despite the ambitions of parents and educators to increase the number, actually continue to college graduation. The fact that some who pursue and attain a college degree may be disappointed in not obtaining a job which uses knowledge and skills gained is not the most damaging impact of the myth. The message, drummed into the subconsciousness of the majority who do not obtain college degrees, is that they are somehow second class. Certainly college education should not be discouraged. It will probably continue to be experienced by more and more American youth. But it must not continue to be advertised as the only acceptable and really effective method of occupational preparation.

While American education is culpable for overemphasizing college as a prerequisite to career success, it is also criticized for pursuing "school for schooling's sake" and ignoring the increasingly close relationships between education and work. Education has assumed too long that the best way to prepare pupils for the real world is to keep them apart from that world. As education becomes more and more a necessary prerequisite for entry into the world of work, the education system can less and less afford to adopt an insular attitude. It is in the elementary school where the basic skills necessary for all kinds of occupational success are supposedly taught. Yet in school after school, both the third grade teacher and her pupils seem to be operating as though their prime reason for being together is to ready students for the fourth grade! The purpose of education simply cannot be more education. Education must be seen as preparation for *something* — both as preparation for living and preparation for making a living.

Another source of criticism is the one-quarter of all students who never graduate from high school. The well-publicized phenomenon of the "high school dropout" is, as most elementary educators well know, only the tip of a much larger iceberg. That is, many more students, while persisting until high school graduation, can find no true meaning in their educational experiences and no really good reason for going to school. Of those who will drop out of high school, more than half can be identified before they complete the fifth grade; i.e., they were "turned off" to the public school system long before they became high school students. Whether we label such students as "unmotivated," as "reluctant learners," or by some others descriptive term, it is obvious that for whatever set of causal reasons, school does not make sense to them. Career education is one of several new approaches holding promise for attacking this condition at its basic roots.

Increasingly, even those who have heeded parental and educator ambitions for them and have obtained the advocated college diploma begin to suspect that they too are the victims of overpromise. For two decades the demand for college-educated manpower to fill professional and technical jobs grew more rapidly than the supply, and the holder of a college degree was in a prime position in the labor market. Now that demand and supply for most such jobs have been brought into better balance — demand having slowed its growth rate and the colleges having achieved overcapacity in supplying most needs — competition has stiffened in such job markets. Employers are in a better position to demand and compare performance, and graduates often find that they have neither the expected job guarantee nor the required competence.

One basic societal concern underlying the call for career education is suspicion that the classical work ethic is being eroded as a vital part of our system of social values. Is the traditional work ethic, called "puritan" or "protestant" for historical reasons, appropriate to an impending post-industrial society? If adherence to it is disappearing, can other more useful and personally meaningful forms of work values be found? Can a society survive without some form of work ethic, even in the present day? These are critical issues for American education.

Too many, even in education, refuse to face up to the critical importance of attitudes toward work in the personal value systems of a people. Some contend that productivity trends, technology, a shorter work week, and a shorter working life all portend the disappearance of work as a vital force in the life-style of future Americans. Nothing could be farther from the truth. Increased leisure is one of the rewards of productivity and depends upon it. Each increment of productivity can be used to buy more goods and services or more leisure, but not both. One cannot sensibly talk about reducing poverty here or abroad, or meeting any of the endless list of social and personal needs, and still expect any disappearance of work. The nature of work is changing and becoming generally less arduous. The rebellion against unchallenging and uninteresting work is not the result of deteriorating working conditions but of relative unattractiveness of stable occupations as the average improves. In his perception, the blue-collar and lower level white-collar worker sees, on the one hand, publicly supported welfare recipients and, on the other, pleasantly employed technicians, managers, and professionals, and believes he is the only one left doing society's menial but necessary tasks.

One source of confusion is the tendency to think of work only in labor market terms. As material abundance increases, an endless list of service needs requiring volunteer effort adds to the total work to be done. Even many advocates of career education do not subscribe to the societal need to maintain a strong work ethic. They complain that there is much more to life than making a living and that career education's role should be assisting in the development of "fully self-actualized individuals."

We believe that those who would argue in such a fashion are wrong. We readily admit that preparation for making a living is only part of preparation for living itself, but we contend that it is a very important part which in the past has not received a high enough priority among the goals of American education. The trends are toward fewer hours spent in work. Nevertheless, both now and in the foreseeable future, most Americans will spend more time working or seeking work than in any other single form of activity. We agree that full self-actualization demands a self-concept more encompassing than that of a worker, but insist that most individuals are best known to themselves and to others through their accomplishments — and that work remains our single most available means of accomplishment.

If some more viable form of the work ethic is to be restored, the American education system in general, and elementary education in particular, has a vital and essential role to play. The work ethic is simply part of a set of personal values related to occupational life that could conceivably give meaning and direction to the life of an individual. It is well known that the strongest and most permanent personal values are those which are developed prior to the time one reaches physical maturity. The elementary school is a powerful force in the shaping of personal values. Today millions of elementary school children are being systematically exposed neither to work values nor to a broad understanding of our rapidly changing world of work. More importantly, they are being given little opportunity to relate such understandings to themselves as their personal value systems develop. The career education movement seeks and is enlisting the help of elementary education in turning this condition around. That is why career education in its most basic form *must* — if it is to be fully effective — begin and have a strong base in the elementary school.

The combination of societal and educational conditions described here have combined to create the current call for career education. What is this new concept that promises an answer to this serious set of problems?

CAREER EDUCATION DEFINED

In one sense, career education already has qualified as a bona fide educational concept; i.e., it has many proponents from a wide variety of disciplines within education. It also has a growing number of skeptics and critics, partly because each of the so-called "leaders" in career education seems to have his own unique definition that he claims is the "real" one.

In late fall 1971, a number of individuals in career education met at a national invitational conference conducted by the Center for Occupational Education, North Carolina State University. Each participant

was asked to submit, in an anonymous fashion, his or her own definition
of "career education." The following examples of definitions submitted
at that conference illustrate the diversity of points of view that currently
exist:

(1) "Career education can be defined as that part of the total school
curriculum which provides the student with the knowledge,
exploratory experiences, and skills required for successful job
entry, job adjustment, and job advancement. It can also be
defined as an organized K–12 [kindergarten through twelfth
grade] program to provide every student with an understanding of and preparation for the world of work."

(2) "Career education may be described or defined as a comprehensive educational program which gives attention to preparing all people for satisfying and productive work in our society."

(3) "Career education is that part of the total education process
which focuses on the successful adaptation of the individual to
the world of work."

(4) "Career education is the systematic development of the natural
powers of a person over his entire lifetime for his life's work.
It involves body, mind, and spirit and is commenced in the
home where the child's will and intellect are nurtured through
love and example by his parents and family members."

(5) "Career education encompasses all education in that it is that
part of a learning experience that assists one to discover, define,
and refine his talents and use them in pursuit of a career."

(6) "The purpose of career education should be to help people
develop human resource competence along with a holistic
understanding of the world of work or wage-employment system; i.e., the socioeconomic institution of working for pay in
modern industrial society — to become *competent* as workers
and *comprehending* as men and women."

These few examples serve to illustrate that the definers of career education differ sharply among themselves with respect to such basic vari-
ables as: (1) the extent to which it is a K–12 or a K–adult program, or
whether it extends from early childhood to retirement, (2) the extent to

which its primary purpose is leading toward work or toward a totally fulfilled life, (3) the extent to which it is all of education or only a part of education, and (4) the extent to which it is an educational program or an entire community program.

The U.S. Office of Education (USOE) has chosen so far to avoid any *official* definition of career education. Instead, USOE policy has consistently stated that career education will in the long run be defined in a grass-roots debate that hopefully will take place throughout the nation. The definitions quoted above illustrate that this debate is now well under way and that there is wide latitude present for differences in opinion.

The nearest that USOE policy statements have come to a definition of career education are found in two places. The first is an article written by USOE Commissioner Sidney P. Marland, Jr., that appeared in the November 1971 issue of *American Education*, in which he said:

> [W]hat the term "career education" means to me is basically a point of view, a concept — a concept that says three things: First, that career education will be part of the curriculum for all students, not just some. Second, that it will continue throughout a youngster's stay in school, from the first grade through senior high and beyond, if he so elects. And third, that every student leaving school will possess the skills necessary to give him a start to making a livelihood for himself and his family, even if he leaves before completing high school.

The second is a May 1971 draft of a document from the Bureau of Adult, Vocational, and Technical Education of USOE titled "Career Education: A Model for Implementation" in which the following definition appears: "Career Education is a comprehensive educational program focused on careers, which begins in Grade 1 or earlier and continues through the adult years."

For our purposes here, it is important to recognize that both of these semiofficial USOE definitions stress the concept that career education must begin in elementary school. This point is deserving of special emphasis.

Without an official definition of career education, anyone has a right to his own, and ours is the following, taken from Kenneth B. Hoyt's definition on page 1 of *Career Education: What It Is and How to Do It:*

> [C]areer education is . . . the total effort of public education and the community aimed at helping all individuals to become famil-

iar with the values of a work-oriented society, to integrate these values into their personal value systems, and to implement these values into their lives in such a way that work becomes possible, meaningful, and satisfying to each individual.

The objectives which mark the way to achievement of the goal of career education, stated in their most simple and direct form, are to help all individuals (a) have reasons to want to work, (b) acquire the skills required for useful work, (c) know how to obtain work opportunities, and (d) enter the world of work as a successful and productive contributor. Career education can be understood only if this set of goals and objectives is kept clearly in mind.

Among the concepts within the realm of this definition, the following are of fundamental significance:

(1) The term "public education" means education available to the public and from which the public may choose. Thus career education is not limited to the K–12 public school system. Rather, it encompasses the public schools, but is extended beyond the twelfth grade to include all of post-secondary education, including community colleges, post-high school occupational education institutions (both public and private), degree-granting colleges and universities, and all adult education.

(2) Career education involves the *joint effort* of public education and the community. It is not something that schools can do by themselves. The school of *hard knocks*, as represented in the broader community, is joining with the school of *hard books*, as represented by the formal education system, to become the total learning environment of career education.

(3) Career education is for all individuals — the very young child and the adults of the community, the intellectually able and the mentally handicapped, males and females, those who will attend college and those who will not, the economically affluent and the economically disadvantaged, and those from rural and those from urban settings.

(4) Career education seeks to help individuals become familiar with the wide variety of work values now present in this society and to choose some set of work values that will be personally

meaningful to each individual. It seeks to impose no single standard form of work values on any individual. While it clearly seeks to help each individual adopt some form of work values, it does not aim to coerce him into doing so.

(5) Career education is vitally concerned with helping individuals *implement* their own personal work values. To do this demands that in addition to *wanting* to work, individuals must also acquire the skills *necessary* to work, and having done this, must then find work that is both meaningful and satisfying to them. Thus jobs, in a generic sense, are not career education's goal. Rather, work as productive activity that holds personal meaning and satisfaction for the individual is the ultimate goal of career education.

THE FIVE COMPONENTS OF CAREER EDUCATION

Our definition in the previous section states career education's objectives and contributors rather than its substance. The child progressing through a career education system during his formative years would traverse five components, each of which is equally essential but which are listed here in order of the extent to which they are a primary responsibility of the schools:

(1) The classroom in which all possible learnings are articulated in terms of the career application for both understanding and motivation

(2) The ultimate acquiring of vocational job skills, whether they are learned on the job, in a structured classroom situation, or from general life experiences

(3) Career development programs for exposure to occupational alternatives and for derivation of a work ethic and a set of work values, allowing the individual to visualize himself in various work settings and to make career decisions which appear to promise the preferred life-style

(4) Interaction among the training institutions, employing institutions, and labor organizations to provide more fertile learning environments than the schoolroom

(5) The home and family from which the individual develops initial attitudes and concepts

These components make varying contributions at what could be considered as four stages of vocational maturation: (1) awareness (ordinarily beginning in the elementary school) to help children become aware of the general nature of the world of work and familiar with the values of a work-oriented society, (2) exploration (a primary responsibility of the middle school or junior high school) during which young people are encouraged to visualize themselves in various work settings and their consequent life-styles and to test the meaning of their various work values, (3) occupational choice (initially tentative, but gaining more specificity in the high school and beyond), and (4) implementation consisting of occupational preparation, placement, and job success. This is not a once-in-a-lifetime process. As new career opportunities open up or come to the attention of an individual, he may cycle through these stages many times in the course of his lifelong career development.

Career education identifies a lengthy set of prerequisites for successful careers and attempts to contribute to their attainment: good mental and physical health, human relations skills, a commitment to honest work as a source of income, and a willingness to accept the discipline of the workplace and to be motivated toward achievement in the work setting. It also requires all of the basic skills of communication and computation and a fundamental familiarity with the concepts of science and technology, as well as a salable skill in demand in the job market. Selection of that skill requires sufficient knowledge of the opportunities available in the labor market to make valid, though tentative, choices and the decision-making skills required for choices. Opportunities to use these skills also require an understanding of the workings of the labor market and an ability to compete successfully in it.

To give substance to the process of career education, each of the five components deserves brief discussion here. Subsequent chapters explore and recommend elementary education's potential and demonstrated contribution to four of the five . . . vocational skills training being excluded for reasons noted below.

A. Role of Educators

Efforts of classroom teachers to emphasize career implications as part of good teaching are a major component in the new career education drama. In brief, this component aims to help students see some relationships between that which they are presently studying and the possible careers they may choose to follow at some future time. As such, it represents a form of educational motivation for the teacher to use *in conjunction with* any other motivational devices that have worked effectively in the past.

Career education does not seek to use this form of educational motivation to replace other effective motivational procedures that classroom teachers have always used. However, this form of motivation should appeal to all students some of the time and to some students almost all of the time. If it is incorporated with all other forms of educational motivation, students could learn more substantive content. For the elementary teacher to emphasize the career implications of substantive content holds great potential for helping all students discover reasons for learning that are directly related to the world of work outside education.

This form of educational motivation is not intended to detract from the actual amount of time students spend in absorbing substantive content. Rather, the *time* required for providing this motivation comes from the total pool of time and effort available to every teacher for pupil motivation. Thus career education in no way seeks to "water down" the substantive content of the elementary school. Instead, it seeks to assure that *more* such content will be meaningfully assimilated by the individual student.

B. *Vocational Skills Training in Formal Education*

The goal of this component is to provide students with occupational skills required to work successfully. The phrase "vocational skills training" rather than "vocational education" is used in part to emphasize the fact that any class may be vocational skills training for one or more of its students. That is, a mathematics class is vocational skills training for the prospective engineer or mathematician or skilled worker, just as a machine shop class is vocational skills training for the prospective machinist. In part, this phrase is used to emphasize the direct and substantial contributions of basic educational skills to occupational competence. That is, we want both students and teachers to recognize that when the student learns to read, he is acquiring skills that will be required for and useful in the work he will eventually pursue as an adult.

We must rid ourselves of the false notion that students do not begin to ready themselves for work until after they leave the elementary school. Moreover, we must rid ourselves of the equally false notion that in the secondary school, only that part called "vocational education" exists to prepare students for work. Most importantly, we must rid ourselves of the false notion that only students who lack the potential for successful college completion are readying themselves for work while they are in our elementary and secondary schools.

Education as preparation for work must become an important goal of all who teach and all who learn. To provide this emphasis adds to the meaning and meaningfulness of all education without in any way detracting from any other worthy educational goal.

Since vocational skills training in the elementary school consists primarily of the acquisition of the standard substantive content of elementary education, it seems neither necessary nor appropriate to devote a chapter of this book to that component. This of course makes the component no less important in the assignment of the elementary teacher.

C. Career Development Programs

This component, involving the efforts of all educators and those of many persons outside education, aims to help students understand themselves in terms of their values, interests, abilities, and accomplishments. Moreover, it seeks to help students see relationships between these kinds of self-understandings and understandings of possible educational-occupational opportunities that are likely to be available to them. Finally, it seeks to help students make some kind of occupational or career decisions based on these kinds of understandings. In short, it represents career education's attempt to emphasize and make meaningful the inherent right of each individual to lead his own life, to control to the maximum extent his own destiny, and to see himself as the worthy and worthwhile person he is.

It should be clear at the outset that during the elementary school years, the career development component seeks no firm occupational commitment on the part of any individual. Rather, it seeks to help the student think about himself in relationship to the world of work and to try to picture himself as a possible contributing member of that world. The elementary school has a key and crucial role to play in this process.

D. Efforts of the Business-Labor-Industry Community

This component assumes that neither students nor educators can learn what they need to know about work or about the relationships between education and work by insulating themselves from the real world of work outside education. Observational work experience and work study opportunities for students and for those who educate students — teachers, counselors, supervisors, school administrators — should be an integral part of the education process.

For elementary school students, this component is implemented primarily through observations of the world of work gained through field trips and through bringing business, industrial, and labor representatives into the elementary school classroom. For the elementary school teacher, this component seeks to provide the teacher with opportunities to gain knowledge regarding the world of work outside education through actual work experience as well as through observations made in that outside world. In part, this component seeks to supply those students who are leaving school for work with the means to make a successful transition from school to work. While this will not be a major concern of the elementary school, it *will* become a part of career education for *some* students.

E. Role of Home and Family

This component recognizes both the right and the responsibility of parents to care about and to influence attitudes which their children develop toward work, toward education, and toward the relationships existing between work and education. It sees the home as a place where work values and the dignity of all honest work can be taught. In addition, it recognizes that if we help students get ready to earn money, we must also help them get ready to spend it, and so assigns a consumer education role jointly to the home and the school. Finally, it recognizes the need to help parents develop and apply means of positively assisting in the career development of their children in ways that will enhance rather than detract from the goals of career education.

Summary

The success of career education is seen as equally dependent upon each of its five major components. Elements of each component have been present in American education for many years. Career education asks that all elements and all components now be put together in a comprehensive career education sequence that will truly make work possible, meaningful, and satisfying to each individual.

Career education is expected to occur in many ways and at many times in the lives of individuals. Its success, at any level and in any setting, is dependent upon the extent to which we can give priority to the individual as our primary concern. Leaders in the career education movement have emphasized repeatedly the necessity for its beginnings during the elementary school years. Most persons making such pronouncements have no clear understanding of what is being asked of the elementary teacher or the extent to which elementary school practices are being requested to change.

The remainder of this book is devoted to specification and clarification of these kinds of understandings. Before the remaining chapters are studied, it seems advisable here to outline in broad form some of the operational problems facing elementary teachers who attempt to change in ways that will make them active and positive contributors to the total career education movement.

Individualization of Instruction

Experienced elementary educators know full well that whenever anyone proposes a new form of educational motivation, he is in fact talking about working with pupils on an individualized basis as much as possible. That is, one doesn't motivate a group, but only individual members of a group. The elementary school classroom that has 30 or more pupils calling for the teacher's attention is simply not conducive to the goal of individualized instruction. We know that many elementary classrooms today have 35 or more pupils. We hear many contending that career education will not be any more expensive in the long run than our current educational programs. This simply is not true. For the classroom teacher to emphasize the career implications of the substantive content she seeks to help pupils learn demands a relatively small class size or an increase in the number of helping adults in the classroom.

There probably is no magic number for the teacher-student ratio. At the same time, there is no point in pretending that career education, in the elementary school, can be truly effective unless concentrated attention is directed toward reducing the teacher-pupil ratio to a point where individualization of instruction can in fact take place.

Increase in Teacher Knowledge

One cannot teach that which he does not know. To ask that elementary teachers help students become aware of and familiar with the world of work outside education demands that teachers themselves become familiar with that world. This cannot be done vicariously or in an incidental manner. It is a particular problem in the elementary school because of the career development patterns followed by many elementary teachers themselves. That is, it is not unusual to find an elementary teacher who has never worked outside the field of formal education except for rather low-level, temporary jobs to help finance his college education. Career education demands that some provision be made for helping elementary school teachers have first-hand experience in the occupational world outside education. This for many teachers is going to mean a twelve-month annual contract with two to three months spent in some form of work experience or work study program. Until teacher education institutions change so that they make such experiences a part of elementary teacher education, the state departments of education and local educational agencies will have to provide the means for this kind of in-service education for elementary teachers. This too is going to cost money.

Need for Coordination of Activities

If career education is seen as a developmental process, then it is important to plan for it in a developmental fashion. What is done in the second grade should not be repeated in the third grade. The variety of career education projects now being proposed to elementary teachers has not, by and large, been specified as belonging at any particular grade level nor in any particular sequence. Elementary school curriculum planners face major problems in planning career education experiences in the elementary school that build on one another and that clearly lead into the career exploration activities planned for the junior high school years. This has been done only sporadically up to this time.

Need for Teacher Cooperation and Planning

Career education in the elementary school seems to be working best in the open space elementary schools. Yet most elementary schools are not yet set up to operate on this basis. Certainly many of the proposed career education activities in the elementary school to be discussed in this book demand a project approach to teaching that involves the coordinated efforts of several teachers. The project approach obviously involves the construction of learning packages. Just as obviously, this takes teacher time and effort. This is not something that can be effectively accomplished in the teacher's "spare" time. It is a problem that must be faced at the beginning.

Need for Special Materials

Two distinctly different kinds of special materials are going to be required for career education in the elementary school. One represents materials in the domain of pupil values and self-understanding. Current programs of elementary school career education have done much better in helping pupils become aware of the world of work than in helping pupils become aware of themselves. While some reasonably good commercially prepared materials are beginning to emerge in this area, the best continue to be those constructed by teachers in local elementary school settings. This too will take time, effort, and a considerable amount of in-service education.

The second kind of special material consists of those used to give elementary school students some actual "hands-on" experience with the tools of the industrial and business world. Very few elementary schools are presently equipped with vocational laboratory facilities. Portable units containing basic tools are becoming increasingly popular, as are exchange programs that allow elementary school students to spend some time in secondary school vocational-technical education facilities. Much remains to be done.

Philosophical Concerns

Many elementary school teachers will be appropriately concerned lest the career education emphasis displace traditional educational values to which they have strong professional and philosophical commitments. Most are predisposed to think of "liberal" education as the ideal and vocational education as illiberal, and there is a tendency to read into the career education movement an intent to make all education vocational. If all of this were true, there would be cause for concern, and there is sufficient reason in some uses of the career education term to be on guard. However, if the definition of liberal education is those formal learning experiences which help the individual understand the society in which he lives and himself in relation to it, reexamine the values of that society, and either reconfirm or modify his commitments to them and gain the skills to function successfully within that society, career education must be part (but not the whole) of liberal education. The best way we can illustrate our concept of the role of career education within formal education and of the latter in the total learning process is by devices shown below.

Vocational education is only part of career education and career education only one of the assignments of the education system. Neither can be successfully pursued solely within the formal education system, but important learnings, skills, and values vis-à-vis work and career (perhaps the most important) develop in the home and community outside the schools. The school curriculum is always overloaded with both objectives and content. The essential task for advocates and designers of a

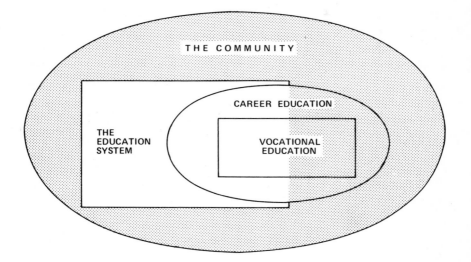

Career Education's Place in Education

greater career emphasis within education is to integrate its values, objectives, and content into the curriculum in such a way that they will supersede nothing which is equally essential and support all that is.

The prime objective and assignment of the elementary school is to aid the development of the whole human being and to supply some of the essential skills of life in society. Career preparation and participation are certainly a vital part of that development and those skills.

Each of these problems, and more, will be discussed in the chapters that follow. They are raised here simply for purposes of identification and awareness. Career education has come to American education. The elementary school has a crucial role to play in career education. The case for career education is strong, and the call for career education is clear. It remains for professional educators at all levels to recognize the challenge of career education and to convert it into effective programs that will accomplish the goals of career education without in any way demeaning or detracting from all other worthy educational goals and objectives.

Suggestions for Further Reading

Janne, Henri. "Teaching People to Adapt to Change." *The Futurist* IV (June 1970) :81.

Hoyt, Kenneth B.; Evans, Rupert N.; Mackin, Edward F.; and Mangum, Garth L. *Career Education: What It Is and How to Do It.* Salt Lake City: Olympus Publishing Company, 1972.

U.S. Office of Education, Bureau of Adult, Vocational, and Technical Education. "Career Education: A Model for Implementation." 1971. Preliminary draft.

White House Conference on Youth: Recommendations and Resolutions. Washington, D.C.: U.S. Government Printing Office, 1971.

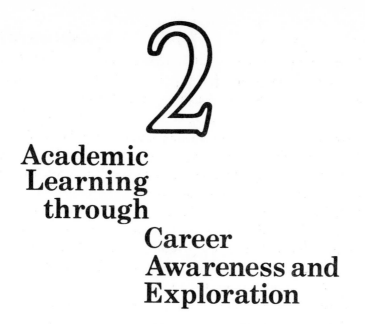

Academic Learning through Career Awareness and Exploration

A key component of career education consists of efforts of all classroom teachers, at all levels of education, to teach career implications of their subject matter. This chapter provides the rationale behind that component, identifies the basic principles inherent in the operational implementation, and presents a variety of examples in actual practice.

RATIONALE

The basic rationale behind this component of career education is a dual objective: that the substantive content of career education and the basic educative skills which form the heart of elementary education can *both* be made most meaningful to pupils if they are taught together. Put another way, it rejects the notion that the substance of career education should be thought of as another subject to be added to the already overcrowded elementary school curriculum.

The component finds motivational advantages inherent in helping students see some relationships between that which they are being asked to learn in the elementary school and the occupational society of which they will ultimately be a part. As a form of educational motivation, the objective of helping students understand the career implications of their subject matter must be tied as closely as possible to the subject matter content of prime concern to the elementary school educator.

Helping pupils understand the career implications of their subject matter represents only one of several forms of educational motivation available to the experienced elementary school teacher. Thus it is not suggested or recommended that in every classroom on every day, career relevance be the only form of educational motivation the teacher should use. However, it does represent a powerful source of educational stimulus which, if added to all others now used by elementary teachers, should help pupils learn more subject matter content.

With this background, it should be clear that the objectives of career education and those of elementary school education merge in the goal of helping each student learn as much subject matter content as he possibly can. Those elementary educators who fear that career education may dilute or take time away from efforts to help pupils master the basic skills of language arts, social studies, science, or mathematics have nothing to worry about if they understand the career education movement.

At the same time, young people — for whom the school hours are often their only organized and directed learning experiences — can be guided into consciously identifying and internalizing concepts about the world of work. This will aid them in building work values and understanding as a basis for future career decision making.

It is first necessary to demonstrate the harmony between elementary education and career education objectives and then to derive principles for building career education learning experiences. Examples can then illustrate this process.

ELEMENTARY SCHOOL OBJECTIVES AND CAREER EDUCATION CONTRIBUTIONS

The elementary school states as its domain that portion of the formal education process dealing with the acquisition of the basic skills we know as reading, writing, and arithmetic. It also begins to impart the cumulative tradition of the past through the study of other peoples, other times, and other places. If the objective of the elementary school has been to provide both the human and processing skills which enable the child to make an effective transition to the next educational setting — that is, coping with more education — the objective of an ongoing career awareness approach is to use existing curriculum and community in the development and maintenance of a positive self-concept as it relates to a synthesis of future work roles. There can be no argument as to the worthiness of these concurrent aims, but it is important to point out the variance in the transitional behavior observable in the child who has been exposed to a thoughtfully designed career education program in the elementary grades. This child *should be able to*

(1) Discuss his interests as they relate to work and play behaviors

(2) Distinguish among people who work with others, ideas, or things

(3) Recognize worker interdependence within the home, the school, and the business community

(4) Make connections between school subjects and employability skills

(5) Role-play or visually depict the worker personality characteristics associated with people who produce goods or services or both

(6) Discuss the likenesses and differences between himself and his family members, his schoolmates, and others who are significant in his life

(7) Consider the many reasons why people work

(8) Attach worth and value to all who work, either for themselves or for others

(9) Display an optimism about himself in direct proportion to the number and quality of direct contacts he makes with people who work

Thus the student career awareness and self-awareness objectives should have been enhanced. But at the same time and as a consequence of this approach, the student should be better able to

(1) Recognize the utility of basic arithmetic skills in situations where he must conserve, spend, and build — *as well as* solve an immediate mathematical task stated as a classroom exercise

(2) Recognize the utility of basic communications skills in situations where he must persuade, defend, inspire, encourage, or translate — *as well as* communicate a given idea

(3) Recognize the utility of basic scientific principles in situations where he must work with, or modify, existing environmental elements — *as well as* test a known scientific formula

(4) Recognize the utility of basic social science principles in situations where he must deal with current social attitudes, habits, and needs — *as well as* articulate a synthesis of the world's cultures

(5) Recognize the utility of basic physiological principles in situations where he must match psychomotor skills with the ongoing maintenance and task appropriateness of those skills — *as well as* achieve mastery over a given physical challenge

Thus, in achieving (1), career education would have made a vital contribution to math; in (2), to language, art, and music; in (3), to science, biology, physics, etc.; in (4) to social studies; and in (5) physical education and health, without adding to the total curriculum load.

In this chapter, our particular concern is with the proposition that academic skills can be acquired with equal or greater facility when they are studied in a career awareness context. The elementary school has special advantages for this application. In later stages of the schooling process, subject matter is specialized by teacher and by classroom; thus career relevance must be related to one subject at a time.

The elementary school setting is distinguished by its capacity to house a daily six-hour investigation of an idea, an action, a person, a group, or an entire culture. The one classroom and the growing intimacy between teacher and children can free curriculum from its restriction to blocks of subject matter by presenting all academic skills as necessary handles to the outside world. To tell the child that these handles exist is not enough; he is entitled to some small proof of them and involvement in them through exercises absorbing him both physically and mentally.

In designing such exercises, the teacher would need to look toward the community where examples of tasks begun and finished exist in terms of the work that people do, in settings devoted to leisure as well as to the production of goods and services. Every child can express more than one citation of "interesting grown-ups I know" . . . and teachers can draw from this bank of possible models a simulated activity or project which faithfully duplicates the texture of a goal or product-oriented task in the community. The classroom then becomes a starting point and a hearing room for those portions of the activity which ultimately necessitate a departure from the classroom. In many projects, children will need to gather first-hand information by entering a part of the working world to play out their drama in authentic surroundings. In others, they will bring the community to the school as consultants to activities involving the immediate school environment. In all such activity, the utility and appearance of basic academic skills will be unmistakable to the teacher and newly relevant to the child.

Contrast the following activities as they might appear to an elementary school child:

	Traditional Approach	*Career Awareness Approach*
PRIMARY MATH	Add six single-digit numbers. Multiply by twos. Subtract single-digit numbers. Count to fifty.	Discuss with students the kinds of information communicated about them by numbers: age, weight, height, clothing sizes, street and telephone numbers, etc. Have them list all those they can. Separate numbers describing physical from social characteristics. Ask each child to build a chart depicting each new symbol he must memorize in order to communicate: *time* for meals and bedtime; *distance* from home to school (blocks, miles); *conservation properties* (more/less, big/small, plus/minus, etc.). He can also keep his own record of weight gain or loss, inches gained, etc. Continue to explore other ways that numbers talk about people — father's driver's license number, brother's Social Security number, etc., and how these accumulate as one grows older.
INTERMEDIATE MATH	If there are twelve apples in a bag, and we take away a third of them, how many apples would be left? Two trains, traveling at 65 mph on parallel	Have the students pretend that they are role-playing the act of taking over the kitchen management of a nearby motel. Have them suggest their favorite recipes for entrees, salads, and desserts. Have them multiply portions so that they can

Traditional Approach	Career Awareness Approach
tracks, are approaching each other. If the trains left simultaneously from their points of departure, 195 miles apart, how far from each city is each train when it passes the other?	serve parents and grandparents of every student. Estimate cost per adult, based on labor, supplies, and profit margin. Follow up this exercise by discussing this as a real project with a locally franchised motel.

PRIMARY LANGUAGE ARTS

Phonics drills. Look-see-say drills. New alphabet technique. Dick and Jane, and others.	Have students role-play the language a parent uses when he or she is a judge, a nurse, a short-order cook, or an accountant, a badminton player, or a carpenter. Draw out occupationally related vocabulary: Judge: yes/no; right/wrong Nurse: sick/well; sleep/play Cook: hot/cold; sweet/sour Accountant: count; add; list Badminton player: play; jump; net Carpenter: fix; nail; hammer

INTERMEDIATE LANGUAGE ARTS

Short stories about pleasant, middle-class families. Drills on content interpretation. Parts of speech; punctuation. Spelling bees. Standardized one-act plays.	Have students dictate their customized revisions of first and second grade mathematics and reading texts into a recorder, after reviewing first and second grade texts. Some students can transcribe, edit, and proofread the written product, while others illustrate booklets. Children present these to first and second graders and work with them on a regular tutoring basis to determine success of their product as well as their own abilities to work effectively with younger children.[1]

PRIMARY SCIENCE

Study of health and hygiene as related to personal habits.	Have students make a chart with columns: Heat, Cold, and Antiseptic. Which household appliances or family practices use each of these methods to retard growth of bacteria (cooking, freezing, cleaning with iodine, storing in dark areas, etc.)?

---

[1] An example of this activity is described in the February 1972 issue of *The Instructor*, wherein the efforts of mother-daughter teaching teams in Buffalo Grove and Skokie, Illinois, are documented.

	Traditional Approach	*Career Awareness Approach*
		Parallel these practices and their uses with medical/health procedures and the workers using them during a sequence of visits to a nearby clinic, hospital, or restaurant.[2]
INTERMEDIATE SCIENCE	Study of physical environment, minerals, plants, and general biology.	Have children contrast and chart *natural* foods, metals, oils, and materials (cotton, wool, leather, etc.) with man-made products or synthetics.[3] Ask speakers who work in agriculture, pharmacy, mining, petroleum, and clothing to speak with children on the pros and cons of technology as it relates to the balance of nature and man's health.
PRIMARY SOCIAL STUDIES	Read the unit on community workers in basal text. Visit firehouse and police station.	Teacher and students take a walking tour of the neighborhood to locate land available for future development. Teacher maps those sites on dittos. What do students see as needs for which these could be used (shopping centers, residential areas, parks, hospitals, etc.)? Discuss *who* would be involved in making and carrying out these decisions. Call representatives whom the children select, and ask them to come to the classroom to hear the children's recommendations.
INTERMEDIATE SOCIAL STUDIES	Study text on other lands, other peoples. Have students bring pictures, bric-a-brac, travel books, and posters which are owned by the family for "show and tell."	Travel by air, rail, sea, and land has caused many jobs to become obsolete, while others have been created. Ask the children to discuss these workers of the past and present whose skills could still serve in a modern transportation system, and how they would reposition those whose specific skills are no longer in demand. Have the students survey local travel agencies as to consumer preference

---

[2] Adapted from the Maryland State Department of Education's "Calling Careers" instructional television teacher manuals.

[3] *Ibid.*

Traditional   *Career Awareness*
Approach   *Approach*

in travel mode, destination, and season. Communicate results of the survey to newspapers in a pilot effort to get a permanent column on topical and human concerns.
How many countries are represented in the grandparent population? Children compile a list and begin correspondence with pen pals given by different embassies they write for information. They begin construction of their own genealogy charts as they correspond with distant relatives.

It will be noted that much of what is described as "traditional" still carries with it the weight of logic and relevancy to the adult reader. Yet, combined with the career awareness orientation, the traditional could assume a full-bodied significance to the young child at that moment when learning takes place. The joy of knowing he has learned could well be the single most important reason why all teachers should and can improve upon these illustrations.

Examples of Academic Learning through Career Awareness

The elementary school's self-contained classroom allows numerous objectives to be pursued simultaneously. Several of career education's components can be combined with the subject matter of a number of academic disciplines in a single project. Since examples of what does or could exist are limitless, a few will suffice. The most successful will be those a particular teacher develops or adapts to the needs of specific students in their environment. The "how to do it" of that is the subject of the next section of this chapter.

A Georgia project seeks to combine the subject matter of health, math, and English with the career education goals of career awareness and academic skills acquisition. For instance, children are video-taped while role-playing the simulated activities of admitting tonsillectomy patients to the hospital. With a "set" established in the classroom, children make blood tests and take x rays, chart vital information and prescribe medication, calm and reassure patient, prep for operation, discuss with fellow "surgeons" a plan by indicating location of surgery on anatomical charts. Actors proceed through recovery room to the patient's room where parents and toys are waiting. Every child has a part to play . . . in predrama research, building sets, obtaining "tools," enacting roles. They show the tapes to other classes and to their hospital "advocate" team for critique and validation.[4]

In Maryland, teams of two students each selected a two-person team of workers (in the school these could be found in the office, in the boiler room, and in the cafeteria; in the home, these could be found in the parents who are involved in repainting the living room, laying carpet tiles, paying monthly bills, etc.) located in school, home, or larger community (here the students could visit local businesses, banks, and warehouses). One student would record each evidence of a math skill or concept being used or discussed, while the other student would record each evidence of occupationally related vocabulary (e.g., blueprints, ledgers, bank statements, carburetors, etc.). Their report to the class summarized the proportions of math and vocabulary skills "used" in each occupation.[5]

After observing the people working in a local bank, Maryland children returned to set up a classroom prototype which rotated them in specific roles of teller, loan officer, accountant, president, security officer, etc. They established a "token" system based on task completion, and used the bank as a repository. The children were instructed on the use of a checkbook so that they might keep records of deposits or withdrawals. Tokens withdrawn were spent on class "privileges" such as independent projects, visits to library or other classrooms, voluntary assistance to school personnel on the grounds or in buildings. Children wishing to draw tokens from an "overdrawn" account were interviewed by the loan officer who, with the "president's" signature, loaned tokens in exchange for a promissory note stating a specific future service by the borrower.[6]

The values of language, art, math, and drama can be combined with career awareness, academic skill acquisition and human relations skills by asking children to communicate in silence for one full day by using

---

[4] Taken from the Cobb County Career Development Project, Marietta, Georgia.

[5] Taken from the Anne Arundel County Career Development Project, County Board of Education, Annapolis, Maryland.

[6] Taken from the Quality Improvement Project, Hickory Elementary School, Bel Air, Maryland.

cards of various colors and shapes to request things of one another and the teacher. On the next day, have the children imagine that they are in a foreign country and do not speak the language, yet are forbidden to pantomime their needs. Present a panel of a commercial artist, a sign painter, a cartoonist, and a portrait artist and let the students question each of them as to how they would help "strangers" find what they wanted. Follow up by having students conduct a silent day for the entire school, using directional signs, numbers, colors, and free art. Write results and send copies to the state roads commission, hospitals, recreation and parks department, locally franchised motels, and newspapers.

An Iowa project drew upon family living for its potential in relating school and work behaviors and skills.[7] Fifth and sixth grade classes were divided into families of three to six members who assessed their own social and skill incomes over a six-month period. Each family was given a proportionate monthly capital from which to operate. From this, the family members determined actuarial minimums of fixed expenses (e.g., housing, taxes, utilities, insurance, etc.) and varying expenses (transportation or car payments, food, recreation, clothing, etc.). Research determined appropriate costs while teaching computation and such concepts as averaging. Capital was deposited in the class "bank" which was operated by four students on a two-month rotating basis. After payment for fixed expenses was made, student families made decisions on how they could allocate varying expenses, spend surplus (if any), and supplement "income" if it was insufficient to support the life-styles of its members. Monthly income was increased as a reward for desirable school behaviors.

Deficit spending was arranged to occur through one or both of two circumstances; e.g., overspending of baseline income and the teacher-imposed crisis or problem of hospitalization, emergency repair, etc., drawn from a stack of cards indicating cases. Families had then to decide whether to create a product to increase income, to perform a "service" for which other families could write a check, or to increase the rewarded behaviors.

The direct association of this suggested theme to all subject matters, to authentic illustrations of future social and economic realities, and to

---

[7] Taken from the Models for Career Education in Iowa; Elementary. Iowa State University and Iowa Department of Public Instruction, Ames, Iowa.

numerous careers which must be investigated in order to establish minimums of survival and maximums of leisure and recreational options has tremendous implication for the elementary school curriculum. Perhaps even more important is the unpredicted learning which will occur when classroom "families" faced with bankruptcy ask their neighbors to respond to creative new services or products. The response of these neighbors — whether conserving through refusing, bartering, suggesting a family merger, or perhaps even overextending their sympathies — can be the occasion for much student insight and learning.

Valuing, knowing, and changing the environment has been the approach found most useful to the staff and students of an elementary school in rural Maryland.[8] Teachers who were assigned to a new open space school emerged from a summer workshop experience with specific statistics about their new student body. They learned that these youngsters perceived themselves as situationally bound to inherit the occupations of their parents, and that these occupations were limited, with a few exceptions, to a handful of agribusiness careers. The teachers also learned that the open school concept requires an almost total readjustment of instructional methodology. In combining these factors with their commitment to an investigation of career education's implications for total curriculum, they resolved upon the logical extension of the open school into the physical environment around it.

Behind the school ran a sizable stream whose banks were rapidly eroding. Not only was the safety of the children a primary concern, the natural beauty of the setting was being threatened by months of neglect. When school began, so did the "Stream Bank" project, which was the genesis of the students' motto: "Stabilize, improve, and learn from the natural world." The plan was drawn up by a task force of teachers, students, and representatives from both local and distant businesses, agencies, and environmental protection groups. From the beginning, students were involved in the design of an outdoor ecology center which was to be the visible result of year-long effort. While other children studied blueprints obtained from the local board of education and were instructed in survey techniques by a local firm, younger children took

---

[8] Taken from the Potomac Heights Elementary School's Stream Bank project, Hagerstown, Maryland.

pictures of the grounds from all angles in order to present a slide-tape to the first PTA meeting scheduled for the fall term.

Meanwhile the state's soil conservation agency representative made recommendations for priority activity in the stream bank's stabilization. Each of these activities was bid upon by the student groups. Options were carefully designed to be appropriate for the maturation levels of the groups, as well as coordinated with the use of basic academic competencies being addressed. Math, science, language arts, social studies, health, physical education, art, and music assignments were all melded around the environmental project. Career awareness and human relations skills were also emphasized.

These beginning activities were jumping off points for students and staff. As the year progressed and concluded, the vision of a major environmental change was indeed realized. But it is important to note that a visitor today would find more than physical changes around the school. Students who are able to see and touch the rewards of inquiry and involvement in curriculum decisions are also capable of extending their horizons beyond an immediate community's configuration of future career roles. Every school and every teacher who opens these doors for young people must also accept the consequence of their going through them — for few will wish to go back.

These approaches can be effective motivations for children, but might pose a problem for those teachers who fear that extensive curriculum modification would have to precede them. To virtually "scrap" existing curriculum guides — and some of these are extremely well done — may be anathema to some teachers. To others, the challenge of customizing existing curriculum to the needs and interests of their students — while still retaining primary focus on the acquisition of basic skills — may represent a welcome freedom from the national norms used by textbook publishers. However, it will be the teachers' own projects, combining elementary education and career education objectives, which will provide that challenge. For that, the process of building career education curriculum must be explored.

Principles in Building Career Education Learning Experiences

The general approach described in this chapter might be called the "career education learning experience." Others use terms such as "learning packages," "simulated activity module," or some other expression. Whatever the phrase, it should be clear that the project-activity approach to instruction is being discussed. This instructional approach is of course neither new nor strange to the elementary school educator. It is only necessary to make explicit the operational principles required to use this approach in an elementary school career education program.

Of first concern is the matter of substantive content. The goal is to combine the substantive content of career education with the substantive content of the academic disciplines as these exist in the elementary school. The operational problem of many elementary school teachers is that they simply do not know the substantive content of career education.

The substantive content of career education consists in part of basic information regarding occupations, the world of work, career development, and the nature of work. In part, the substantive content of career education consists of career education concepts that pupils should have assimilated by the time they leave the elementary school. Such concepts grow out of the basic knowledge referred to above. Essentially, it is a matter of translating major generalizations concerning work, occupations, careers, and career development into terms that can serve as teacher goals. Many such concepts can and have been developed around a wide variety of areas. The following list, while not comprehensive, illustrates the kinds of career education concepts that could be formulated for use in the elementary school.

Concepts Related to the Role of Work in Life and Society

(1) At least some people must work if society is to survive.

(2) Society is dependent upon the work of many people.

(3) All work needed by society is honorable and dignified.

(4) Trained, experienced, productive workers are more useful and more in demand than untrained, inexperienced, or nonproductive workers.

(5) Man's work determines his standard of living.

(6) Work provides opportunities for one to enhance his dignity and worth.

(7) There is a relationship between the commitment to education and work and the availability and enjoyment of leisure time.

(8) The individual's perception of people affects his ability to work cooperatively.

(9) Job satisfaction is dependent on harmonious relationships between a worker and his work environment.

(10) The economic system structures incentives for man to work.

(11) Our economic system influences work opportunity.

(12) Job specialization creates interdependency.

Concepts Related to the Nature of the World of Work

(1) Some workers produce goods; others produce services.

(2) There is a wide variety of occupations that may be classified in several ways.

(3) There are job clusters within occupational areas, as well as across occupational areas.

(4) Any career area has different levels of responsibility.

(5) Society enacts laws to protect the individual as a producer and consumer of goods and services.

(6) The customs, traditions, and attitudes of society affect the world of work.

(7) Technological developments cause a continual change in the emergence and disappearance of jobs.

(8) The pace of technological development has been accelerated in recent times.

(9) Man must learn to use technology to his advantage.

Concepts Related to Work Values

(1) People work for various rewards and satisfactions.

(2) Work that is enjoyed by some people is disliked by others.

(3) Work means different things to different people.

(4) Generally, those workers who are trained, experienced, and productive find their work satisfying.

(5) Occupations and life-styles are interrelated.

(6) Persons need to be recognized as having dignity and worth.

(7) The individual's perception of his environment affects his attitudes toward work.

Concepts Related to Education and the World of Work

(1) Education and work are interrelated.

(2) Different kinds of work require varying degrees and types of educational preparation.

(3) Basic education enhances job performance.

(4) There are both specific and general knowledges for each career area.

(5) There are many training routes to job entry.

(6) Workers may need vocational retraining several times in the course of a lifetime.

(7) Knowledge and skills in different subjects relate to performance in different work roles.

Concepts Related to Career Development and Career Decision Making

(1) Every individual can have a meaningful, rewarding career.

(2) Individuals differ in their interests, aptitudes, abilities, values, and attitudes; and occupations differ in their requirements and prospects.

(3) Career planning should be a privilege and responsibility of the individual.

(4) The understanding, acceptance, and development of self is a lifelong process and is constantly changed and influenced by life experiences.

(5) Environment and individual potential interact to influence career development.

(6) Hobbies and interests may lead to a vocation.

(7) Occupational supply and demand has an impact on career planning.

(8) Work experience facilitates career decision making.

(9) Individuals can learn to perform adequately in a variety of occupations.

(10) Every career requires some special preparation.

(11) Job characteristics and individuals must be flexible in a changing society.

(12) A person's relationships with other people, with his employer, and with society affect his own career, as well as the careers of others.

Concepts Related to Work Habits

(1) A worker must understand not only his job, but also his employer's rules, regulations, policies, and procedures.

(2) There are identifiable attitudes and behaviors which enable one to obtain and hold a job.

Using the Career Education Concepts

Having derived a set of such concepts, the elementary school teacher is faced with the problem of trying to emphasize these concepts in ways that will help pupils learn more subject matter. The career education learning experience is the vehicle for doing so. There are three essential ingredients involved: (a) the subject matter, (b) the career education concept, and (c) the activities to be included in the career education learning experience. Teachers will be most successful if they are encouraged to build this learning experience in ways that leave them free to begin with any one of the three essential ingredients. It matters little whether the teacher begins with a concern for subject matter, for a career education concept, or with an interest in a particular kind of prepared student activity. On the other hand, it matters greatly that all three ingredients are clearly present in the completed career education learning experience.

It is obvious that the most unfamiliar ingredient to the typical elementary school teacher will be the career education concepts. Thus it is essential that such concepts be developed or adopted by teachers in ways that are meaningful to them. For most schools, this will require an inservice education effort such as described in chapter 6. Once the major concepts to be incorporated into the elementary program are known to and understood by those teachers who will be building the career education learning experiences, it is not at all unusual to find teachers proposing many subconcepts that are meaningful and important to them. This is a most desirable practice. Career education concepts are not automatically meaningful to teachers. Yet it is essential that they become so if the teacher is to develop a good learning experience for the students.

There is a natural inclination for teachers, when looking at a particular set of career education concepts, to think that either (a) all of the concepts should be covered at each grade level, or (b) the concepts should be divided so that some are taught at each of the grade levels. In general, it is not initially productive to opt for either of these approaches. Instead, each teacher should pick a concept the teacher considers important for pupils to understand. As time goes on and more and more learning experiences are developed, the staff will find that all of the concepts are covered — and sometimes several times — at each grade level. It is much more important for teachers to develop learning experiences that are personally meaningful and important to them than to worry about whether all are covered when the program begins.

An additional difference between a career education learning experience and many other teacher-devised activity projects lies in the extent to which the business-labor-industry community is used in project activities. This important topic is discused in chapter 4.

The career education learning experience concept is similar to many project activity approaches to teaching that elementary school teachers are already using in that it typically involves more than one academic skills area. It is of course of central importance that the specific academic skills to be developed in each area be clearly identified as part of the written learning experience. One major weakness of many efforts to develop such experiences is the tendency of some elementary school teachers to ignore, underemphasize, or fail to capitalize fully on opportunities to incorporate academic skills from several subject matter areas into their learning experiences. This seems to occur very often when teachers begin with an idea for a project activity that they think will be interesting for their pupils to follow and that may have direct career implications.

To build a career education learning experience without paying careful attention to the academic skills to be mastered during the project is to defeat one of the most important reasons for the whole career education movement. Two basic principles must be kept constantly in mind: (a) not taking time from imparting subject matter, and (b) using increases in student achievement as one criterion for evaluating the effectiveness of the career education program.

It cannot be too strongly emphasized that the most effective way to help pupils see the career implications of their subject matter is to let each teacher develop his own set of learning experiences. The reasons for emphasizing this point are numerous and include:

(1) The individual teacher is the operational expert best qualified to know where pupils are now in terms of academic skills development and then to determine both the nature and level of skills to be built into the career education learning experience.

(2) Opportunities to use careers and kinds of workers in a particular learning experience vary tremendously from school to school. That which is appropriate in one school might not be appropriate in another.

(3) The activities that form the central planning core of the career education learning experience are most enthusiastically endorsed by the teacher who invented them.

The student will gain more if each teacher can use his own learning experiences as his own "invention." Granted, teachers develop many ideas for building these learning experiences from looking at those which others have developed; but a really dynamic program cannot be developed by trying to take what a different teacher in a different neighborhood — with a different class of students — found ideal, and assume that it is "transportable" across the country. However, other team members can help develop the learning experiences by making suggestions. This process is described in chapter 6.

Finally, something should be said regarding opportunities to teach good work habits as an integral part of the career education learning experience. Project activities do involve *productive efforts* on the part of students that can, in a very real sense, be seen as work. Students can learn more and better work results when good work habits are used. This is one of the "hidden benefits" of the career education learning experience approach that too many teachers have failed to use.

With these general remarks, we can now turn to some illustrative examples of career education learning experiences that practicing elementary school teachers have already developed for each grade level. These examples can be adapted and used wherever they meet the needs of a teacher and students. However, far more will be needed by every teacher. Hopefully, these will act as stimuli for teachers to develop their own experiences, integrating the teaching of academic subjects in their own way. In each of the examples, there is a section which asks: "What curriculum areas were incorporated into the experience? How?" Each teacher should make an attempt to incorporate these suggestions into each learning experience that is developed.

KINDERGARTEN EXPERIENCES

Visiting Highway Patrolman

1. *Major concept:* All jobs contribute to society.
2. What curriculum areas were incorporated into the experience? How?
   a. Language — listening and discussion skills
   b. Health and safety — discussion of bike safety
   c. Social studies — learning about jobs society creates
3. Objectives to be met:
   a. To show how the father of one of the students in the class earns his living, and to demonstrate, through contact, that what he does is important not only to his family and society, but to himself
   b. To show the children how this kind of job helps people obey laws
   c. To help students become aware of how they can participate in personal safety, bike safety, etc.
   d. Children to name one skill a patrolman must have for his job
4. Preparation required (steps or discussions leading into experience):
   a. Contacted father, highway patrolman, and explained what the purpose of this visit to the class would be, and scheduled a time.
   b. Had continuing discussion with the class of the importance of all jobs to our society, and stimulation of children's curiosity to find out about more jobs.
5. Describe the experience:
   Child introduced her father, a highway patrolman, and told the class what she liked best about his job (his hat). He talked about his uniform, duties, and education, and discussed bike safety with the class by reading from a pamphlet he had brought. He then took out small

groups to touch, feel, and hear (siren) and answer their questions about his equipment.

6. Resource people used:
    a. Officer from highway patrol
    b. Career education specialist

7. What other concepts were incorporated into the experience?
    a. Increased self-knowledge and knowledge of the world of work
    b. Learning education requirements

Visiting the Dentist

1. *Major concept:* All jobs contribute to a society.

2. What curriculum areas were incorporated into the experience? How?
    a. Question and discussion skills — talking with the dentist
    b. Cutting and manual manipulation skills — making a book
    c. Language — role-playing techniques
    d. Dental health — tooth care and brushing, proper diet, snack foods vs growing foods

3. Objectives to be met:
    a. Name one reason they would like to be a dentist, and one reason they would not.
    b. Learn dentist's reasons for becoming a dentist.
    c. Better understand reasons for tooth care.
    d. Reduce fear of going to the dentist.
    e. Name three foods which cause decay.
    f. Name three foods which are healthful.

4. Preparation required (steps or discussions leading into experience) (the teacher prepared the class through discussion and films):
    a. "White Teeth, Bright Teeth"
       "Visiting the Dentist"
    b. Book-text from American Dental Association workbook, brush and toothpaste
    c. Large-size samples of dentures and magic toothbrush, toy dental unit for role-playing

5. Describe the experience:

Dentist and his assistant visited the class, arriving with two bags — one which had all the foods which could cause cavities, the other carrying healthful growing foods. They gave the children the opportunity to select from the bags and discuss their choices. Dentist talked about his job, and his assistant about hers. They also gave out pamphlets. One week later, four children visited dentist's office to bring a book the class had constructed. He talked to them, explaining the work he was doing on a patient. Then his assistant showed the students the rest of the office and demonstrated the equipment, allowing the children to handle and manipulate the utensils.

6. Resource people used:

a. Women's dental auxiliary puppet show

b. Dental assistant

c. Dentist

7. What other concepts were incorporated into the experience?

a. Increased self-awareness and knowledge of the world of work

b. Learning of training required for the job

c. Being aware of the contribution of the job to society

d. Naming things they like and do not like about the job

First Grade Experiences

Pottery Lab

1. *Major concept:* It is important to learn about one's self and to learn about the world of work.

2. What curriculum areas were incorporated into the experience? How?

a. Question formulation and listening skills

b. Language — construction of a story chart about what they saw

c. Math — instructor telling of the importance of math in making up the glazes and doing the firing, and giving examples of math problem for the class to solve

3. Objectives to be met:

a. Through visual and tactile senses — experience pottery making on a larger scale (subject matter objective).

    b. Name (from experience this time) two ways pottery is made (occupational information objective).

    c. Tell about facilities needed (kiln) for its completion (occupational information objective).

    d. From watching — tell about how pottery is thrown (concept objective and subject matter objective).

4. Preparation required (steps or discussion leading into experience):

    a. This experience was planned in conjunction with the experience of making small pots, in class.

    b. Class discussed purpose of pottery class at junior college — as a leisure-time activity and observing difference in hand and wheel method of construction.

    c. Teacher made arrangements for first grade to visit an advanced class.

5. Describe the experience:

The class visited the junior college advanced pottery class and had an opportunity to see pottery being thrown and mistakes being made, and to ask questions of the junior college students. They saw clay and pots at different stages of construction and were allowed to handle the clay and bisque pots. Their own teacher — to give them an idea of throwing on a wheel — guided a few children's hands in that experience. He explained the function of the kilns and told how pots are glazed and fired.

6. Resource people used:

Junior college pottery instructor

7. What other concept or concepts were incorporated into the experience?

Identify pottery as an occupation or leisure-time activity in which the person has had experience and in which he might do well and enjoy.

Visiting Father with Tools

1. *Major concept:* It is important to learn about one's self and to learn about the world of work.

2. What curriculum areas were incorporated into the experience? How?

   a. Dexterity skills — working with hands

   b. Spelling — new spelling words from names and uses of tools

   c. Math — measuring distances and seeing dimensions

   d. Language — construction of story chart about experience, in a follow-up manner

3. Objectives to be met:

   a. Name five different tools used in construction.

   b. Describe two tools and how they are used.

   c. Have the opportunity to explore the use of tools, with guidance.

4. Preparation required (steps or discussions leading into experience):

   a. This experience is part of the series to expand awareness of self and world of work.

   b. Different types of dwellings and their construction were discussed as a unit in history and geography. In conjunction, the class discussed what types of tools are used in construction.

   c. The principal visited the class with a blueprint of the school to show the students the importance of plans in relation to construction.

5. Describe the experience:

   A father of one of the students visited the class with his selection of tools to explain and demonstrate their uses. The teacher had on hand various sizes and shapes of scrap wood with which the children were allowed to experiment, using the various tools: hammer, saw, screws, drill, screwdriver, measuring tape, and level.

6. Resource people used:

   Carpenter

7. What other concept or concepts were incorporated into the experience?

   a. Developed self-awareness and increased knowledge of world of work.

   b. Skills learned in school relate to those needed for a job.

SECOND GRADE EXPERIENCE

Dog Trainer — Visiting Parent

1. *Major concept:* Leisure-time activities contribute to personal satisfaction and sometimes develop into paying jobs.

2. What curriculum areas were incorporated into the experience? How?
   a. Question and discussion skills
   b. Writing and spelling — thank-you note
   c. Math — counting, then adding up the different pets the woman
   had

3. Objectives to be met:
   a. Name two reasons why people have hobbies.
   b. Name two things an animal raiser/trainer should have for his
   hobbies — facilities, interest, money, time, etc.
   c. Tell what you would like best about raising dogs.
   d. Tell what you would like least about raising dogs.

4. Preparation required (steps or discussions leading into experience):
   a. Class had visited a pet store as a previous experience.
   b. Teacher discussed with class the types of hobbies and what can be
   gained through hobbies.
   c. Children thought of questions they would ask.
   d. Class discussed standards of conduct around visitor and animals.
   e. Teacher and children made arrangements for a parent/trainer to
   come to class with animal.

5. Describe the experience:

   Woman brought three of her dogs to class, each at a different stage of
   growth and training. She explained how the family became interested
   and started raising and showing dogs, beginning as a hobby and
   becoming a business. She also identified the types of dogs, their care,
   and the facilities necessary for such a hobby. She showed pictures
   and trophies from shows and the children asked questions.

6. Resource people used:

   Dog trainer

7. What other concept or concepts were incorporated into the experience?

   Through discussion:

   a. It is important to like what you do.

   b. Leisure-time activities contribute to personal satisfaction.

   c. Personal satisfaction is important to career development.

8. Follow-up:

   Class discussed what they had learned, their own hobbies, and possible future ones, and wrote thank-you notes.

THIRD GRADE EXPERIENCES

Public Utilities

1. *Major concept:* Individuals must adapt to a changing society.

2. What curriculum areas were incorporated into the experience? How?

   a. Listening and investigation skills

   b. Reading — of brochures

   c. Science and math — in explanation of principles of electricity

3. Objectives to be met:

   a. Name three sources of electrical power.

   b. Name three jobs offered by the local gas and electric company.

   c. Name ten electrical appliances in home.

   d. Name five jobs that would be impossible without electricity.

   e. Name ways in which the jobs in the gas and electric company have changed and how workers could face these changes.

4. Preparation required (steps or discussions leading into experience):

   Three students in class had fathers with the gas and electric companies come to class and discuss their jobs. The paraprofessional contacted the company representative to arrange for truck and a crew, including one of the fathers, to come to school to demonstrate and explain equipment and job.

5. Describe the experience:

   Truck and a three-man crew demonstrated line equipment and explained some of the job's techniques. Students asked questions spontaneously. In demonstrating some of the equipment, one of the crew used a measuring tape to measure distance, thus illustrating how math is used. The following week, a company representative brought a film and some brochures and explained the basic principles of electricity and offered information about the many types of jobs included in the operations. He stressed the importance of education to a prospective worker, and answered student questions.

6. Resource people used:

Public relations personnel and line crew.

7. What other concept or concepts were incorporated into the experience?

   a. Individual must adapt.

   b. College education had not previously been, but is now required.

   c. The grasp of science concepts was seen as important.

8. Follow-up:

Students read and studied public utility brochures and then made up questions for each other concerning various impacts of the public utility in the community.

Post Office

1. *Major concept:* There is an interrelationship between jobs.

2. What curriculum areas were incorporated into the experience? How?

   a. Language — spelling, writing of letters, writing in preparation of questions

   b. Art — drawing some of the machines seen, or pictures of stamps

   c. Social studies — study of Germany (received answers to letters written, and samples of money and stamps)

   d. Questions and discussion skills

3. Objectives to be met:

   a. Name three jobs done at the post office.

   b. Describe three jobs and tell their relationship.

   c. Name two jobs and describe the education of training required for both.

  d. Tell about two machines and their function.

  e. Name two functions of the post office.

4. Preparation required (steps or discussions leading into experience):

  a. During a study of Germany, the students wrote letters to American servicemen's children in the third grade in Germany.

  b. Class discussion of the importance of the post office and its functions.

  c. Kinds of jobs done in the post office and student's preconception of education needed.

  d. Discuss the role of machines, as opposed to 20 years ago.

  e. Prepare questions to ask on tour.

5. Describe the experience:

  Students brought their letters to Germany to be mailed, and upon entering the post office, bought stamps for them. On a guided tour, they watched their letters being canceled, and followed the route in which their letters were taken through the post office. Many of the machines were in operation, causing excitement and activity. The guide described the jobs of the workers seen and explained the various operations taking place. The students asked both spontaneous and prepared questions.

6. Resource people used:

  a. Tour guide and other post office personnel

  b. Career education specialist

7. What concept or concepts were incorporated into the experience?

  a. Increased occupational awareness creates career interest and development.

  b. Interrelationship of work structures and contribution to society.

  c. Increased self-knowledge and job awareness.

FOURTH GRADE EXPERIENCES

Nature Awareness

1. *Major concept:* An individual's interest makes possible a choice of occupations or hobbies.

2. What curriculum areas were incorporated into the experience? How?

   a. Science — bird and insect classification

   b. Ecology — through observation — gaining greater understanding of life-cycles

   c. Science — through observation — noting the interaction of plants and animals

   d. Reading, writing, and spelling — keeping notebooks on information gathered

3. Objectives to be met:

   a. Name and identify four trees native to this area and describe conditions for their growth.

   b. Name and identify three birds.

   c. Name and identify three insects.

4. Preparation required (steps or discussions leading into experience):

   Schools participating in the outdoor education program involve their fourth graders in a week of nature participation. Study and excursion were lead by knowledgeable teachers and included numerous nature walks to gain information about the life-cycles of plants and animals and the interrelationship of nature's creatures, including man's effects on and responsibilities to the environment.

5. Describe the experience:

   Class-size study groups participated in observation, recording, and discussion of information gained about plant and animal life on nature walks, stream investigation, and survival training. The paraprofessional accompanied one of the study groups on such a nature walk, which was a fairly sophisticated biological study of the environmental life encountered on the walk. The students were asked to observe various situations and draw conclusions about what they saw. Visual and audio awareness was encouraged. Flora and fauna were identified.

6. Resource people used:

   a. The fourth grade teacher, former student of zoology and employee of the Fish and Game Department

   b. Participant in outdoor education program

    c. Bird watcher, and someone who appreciates the outdoors

    d. Career education specialist

7. What other concept or concepts were incorporated into the experience?

Through the outdoor education program, many students are afforded the opportunity (which they might not otherwise have had) to come within intimate contact of nature and gain information about her workings. In some students, this may awaken an interest and curiosity which causes them to further the knowledge they gain from this experience and expand it into either a hobby or an occupation, through the perusal of scientifically oriented courses in school, or outside study or training. Creation of interest in a satisfying, possible, leisure-time activity.

Mail Order Catalog

1. *Major concept:* Certain skills are necessary for many jobs.

2. What curriculum areas were incorporated into the experience? How?

    a. Math — totaling cost and weight, using adding machine

    b. Reading — cataloging information

    c. Language — letter writing and addressing of envelopes (the class had been practicing this skill, and the opportunity provided a realistic experience for the skill)

3. Objectives to be met:

    a. Learn to fill out order form.

    b. Learn use and operation of adding machine.

    c. Learn how to use tax table.

    d. Learn to read for information; i.e., what is the required information for the order form.

    e. Total items with tax correctly.

    f. Total weights of merchandise ordered.

    g. Write thank-you letters.

4. Preparation required (steps or discussions leading into experience):

    a. Cut pages from Sears catalog to be used in math.

    b. Duplicate order form from center of catalog.

    c. Mount tax table for opaque projector.

    d. Contact Sears Catalog Department to arrange visit.

    e. Arrange transportation.

5. Describe the experience:

The class took one page of Sears catalog from the boys and girls clothing section. The students selected the items they would like to buy, determined the color, size, and weight. They then filled out an order form for the items; totaled the cost and weight, and used a scale to determine the tax. They checked their totals with the use of the adding machine. After this classroom experience, the students were curious as to how the Catalog Department actually operates, so a visit to Sears was organized to see how the orders are kept straight, handled, and picked up.

6. Resource people utilized:

Manager, mail order catalog department

7. What other concept or concepts were incorporated into the experience?

The manager explained changes in the ordering department and why they were necessary. Technology affects job change. Skills used in filling out order forms were the same as those used on the job by the telephone operators receiving orders. Certain skills are necessary for many jobs.

FIFTH GRADE EXPERIENCES

Commercial Artist

1. *Major concept:* An individual's interest and abilities make possible a choice of occupations or hobbies.

2. What curriculum areas were incorporated into the experience? How?

    a. Art — cartoon character drawn to scale

    b. Math — drawing to scale involving math

    c. Listening and discussion skills

3. Objectives to be met:

    a. Name three possible sources for an artist's ideas.

    b. Name four kinds of media he would have to have knowledge of.

    c. See that art can be a hobby, or an occupation, into which energy is put and satisfaction is derived.

    d. Draw a cartoon figure to scale.

4. Describe the experience:

A commercial artist visited the fifth grade class, bringing examples of some of his completed work, and also the processes by which he arrived at the finished product. He explained the various media he used, special techniques, and the origin of some of his ideas. He talked about personal satisfaction in relation to time and effort required, and self-expectation. The class asked questions. He then drew some candid sketches for the class. A movie was shown — "People Who Make Things" — depicting the interest, energy, and satisfaction of three people in their chosen fields.

5. Resource people used:

    a. Commercial artist

    b. Film — "People Who Make Things"

6. What concept or concepts were incorporated into the experience?

    a. Individual interest and abilities make possible a choice of occupations or hobbies.

    b. Increased knowledge of world of work.

    c. One's work helps to determine his life-style.

7. Follow-up:

Class chose a cartoon character and drew it to scale. This exercise involved math — the use of the ruler and figuring the specifications.

Rocketry

1. *Major concept:* Technology affects job availability.

2. What curriculum areas were incorporated into the experience? How?

    a. Social science — research of Viking shop models and craft of other explorers

    b. Science — research on flight, rocketry, the compass, stars, currents, gravity, earth

    c. Language arts — writing of information gathered

d. Math — calculation of size, time, and distance in relation to craft used for exploration

e. Art — construction of various models

3. Objectives to be met:

a. Name two types of fuel used in rockets.

b. Name five ways man has been able to use a power (manpower, steam power, etc.) in transportation.

c. List six of the types of vehicles man has used for exploration.

d. Be able to understand that two important components of man's exploration depend upon his curiosity and imagination.

4. Preparation required (steps or discussions leading into experience):

a. Movies and books shared on the history of aviation and rocketry.

b. Study and discussion about explorations of yesterday and explorations of today (space programs, ocean environment, Antarctica).

d. Located (after a number of phone calls) a qualified person to come to class to talk about rockets.

d. Discussed with an army colonel our career education program and the kinds of information we are interested in.

5. Describe the experience:

a. Two students constructed a CO_2 cartridge rocket.

b. Teacher explained how the rocket was powered.

c. Students demonstrated the rocket for the class.

d. Colonel came with a film and talked about U.S. guidance systems and answered questions.

6. Resource people used:

a. Military public relations man

b. Two students — in construction of rocket

7. What other concept or concepts were incorporated into the experience?

a. Studying about various explorers would involve recognizing their successes, decisions, and failures as affecting peoples' lives.

    b. Studying exploration from the standpoint of the changes it effects on the way people live and the work they perform; also, following technological progress through the centuries.

    c. Increasing knowledge of world of work.

8. Follow-up:

Boys involved in rocket-making wrote report of their activity.

SIXTH GRADE EXPERIENCE

Cement Plant Operations

1. *Major concept:* Individuals differ in their interests and aptitudes, and this affects job choice.

2. What curriculum areas were incorporated into the experience? How?

    a. Math — students used the slide rules, given the dimensions of an area to be laid with cement, to determine the number of yards of concrete needed.

    b. Math — using the certified weight of their total weights, the children added their weights back in class to check the total, and to determine the average weight for the group.

    c. Speech — language — student made oral report to class on return.

3. Objectives to be met:

    a. Name four components of the concrete mixture.

    b. Name two state requirements for the gravel (cleaners and specific size).

    c. Describe the route of the raw sand with gravel when it is dredged up until it is taken to the plant in specific form.

    d. Name two requirements for men working at the plant.

    e. Name one reason why they would like the job of working at the plant.

    f. Name one reason why they would not like the job at the plant.

    g. Tell two ways the job contributes to society.

4. Preparation required (steps or discussions leading into experience):

   a. While involved in a math unit on cubic measure, some of the class became interested in a discussion of how concrete is measured.

   b. Ten students were interested in visiting a concrete plant.

   c. The teacher contacted a ready-mix concrete company and discussed with the manager questions the students would have, and what the company could offer in the way of a tour. She discussed the level of understanding of the students and related concepts they could grasp in this field.

5. Describe the experience:

   Ten students who were concerned with learning about the workings of this industry were met by the executive manager who described his job in relation to the concrete business. The students then went with him to the plant location where the operations begin. The students were driven to the site of the dredging, where the impure mixture of sand and gravel is brought up from 50 feet below the water surface by crane and then moved by huge earthmovers to be cleaned and separated, according to specification. The students watched and learned about these large machines and then followed the operation to the site where the sand and gravel are segregated by sets of sized screens and piled according to state specification. The manager continued his explanation of the operation, also describing historical methods of weights and measures, facts of weight and measure about the cubic yard, reasons for the necessity of specific measurements. He described some of the jobs done at the plant, their pay scale, and training requirements. After seeing the route of the raw sand and gravel to the cleaned and separated forms, the students then returned with the manager to the plant where the sand and gravel is stored, ready to be mixed in a certain ratio, according to size, with cement and water, to form a cohesive material. The students were given special slide rules to figure the number of yards of concrete mixture needed to fill a given area. The students were then weighed on the truck scale and given a certified weight. With these math ideas in mind, they returned to class to do some figuring and reporting to the rest of the class. Throughout the experience, the students asked questions.

6. Resource people used:

   a. Manager of a concrete plant

   b. Career education specialist

7. What concept or concepts were incorporated into the experience?

   a. Individuals differ in their interest — appreciate both good and bad points of job.

   b. Concept of how job related to, and contributes to society.

   c. Learned training requirements for jobs.

Where People Live

1. *Major concept:* There is a relationship between the type of occupation and the worker's residence location.

2. What curriculum areas were incorporated into the experience? How?

   a. English — discussion, interview, and communication techniques.

   b. Spelling — learning new spelling words from job types and job descriptions.

   c. Social studies — information gained showed the relationship between occupation and residence address.

3. Objectives to be met (concept, occupational information subject matter):

   a. Students to interview each visitor to find out: (a) job description, (b) training and duties, (c) address.

   b. Students to categorize each job encountered into one of three defined areas.

   c. Students to see what the correlation is between type of occupation and workers' residences.

   d. Students to name two possible factors in the relationship between occupation and residence; i.e., salary/house cost, location/convenience to work.

   e. Name two ways the occupation contributes to society.

   f. Name three jobs studied in each category and tell about their interrelationships and similarities. The job clusters can be used in comparison here.

4. Preparation required (steps or discussions leading into experience):

  a. Teacher obtained a large map of the area and had the students put it up in the classroom.

  b. Teacher obtained quantities of six differently colored map tacks.

  c. Class discussion to form a workable definition of white- and blue-collar workers; white to include business and professional positions, blue to include manual occupations; a third category to be service occupations.

  d. Students to name two possible factors in the relationship between occupation and residence; i.e., salary/house cost, location/convenience to work.

  e. Name two ways the occupation contributes to society.

  f. Name three jobs studied in each category and tell about their interrelationships and similarities. (The job clusters can be used in comparison here.)

5. Describe the experience:

To begin the experience, the students first interviewed their father or mother to gain a better understanding of their parents' jobs and to practice fitting the jobs into the described area. Some parents came to class to tell about their jobs. The students worked in small groups to practice job classification, using the categories established in preparation number 4. The students decided on three additional colors to designate their parents' jobs in each of the three areas to correspond to the original color code. Each student then placed the appropriately colored tack at his or her address. A discussion followed as to the similarities or differences of the jobs. Of each visitor, the students asked the job description and salary (if the party didn't mind saying), his training and duties, and his address. A student then placed a colored tack in the proper place, after the class had decided into which category it fit. As the map was developing and at the end of the year, the class discussed the possible relationships between the types of jobs studied, their salaries, and where the worker lived.

6. Resource people used:

  a. Career education specialist in getting various workers to speak to the class

    b. *Occupational Outlook Handbook* used to acquaint the teacher and students with many kinds of jobs and how they can be classified

    c. Various businessmen and community members, including parents

7. What other concept or concepts were incorporated into the experience?

    a. Environment and individual potential interact to influence career development.

    b. Knowledge and skill in different subjects relate to performance in different work roles.

    c. There is a wide variety of occupations which may be classified in several ways.

    d. Societal expectation influence the nature and structure of work.

These illustrations are a few of 300 that were developed in one year's time in Sonoma County, California. They are documented here not as models, but as examples of how some teachers have merged the objectives of elementary and career education. Their intent is to stimulate teachers to create their own projects to teach.

Teaching subject matter areas through career education make academic subjects more relevant. The process used to tap the creative potential of the teachers to develop such experiences will be discussed in a subsequent chapter.

Conclusion: Elementary Education Contributions of Career Education

To teach academic skills in a career awareness setting may involve innovations in the way teachers teach, but not in the way students learn. Each youth learns far more before he enters school and in his daily contacts outside school (after he has reached school age) than he learns during school hours in the classroom. How did he learn before entering the discipline of the classroom? His body — and what he did with it — was his identity. Most of what he did and felt depended upon his ability to interpret or express the relationships of other bodies to his own. The processing of these human encounters occurred with relatively few obstructions during that period educators describe as preschool, yet the breadth and variety of these child-to-people contacts are later discounted by school-based personnel as insignificant or inappropriate modeling experiences.

By the time a child enters kindergarten, this broad acquisition of specific and human reference points (in effect, his placement of himself in the scheme of things) undergoes a radical transformation. In exchange for this membership in a knowledge-seeking corporate body, he must learn to live with less privacy, more insulation from unplanned encounters, and with a bewildering array of unfamiliar objects. His energies are diverted from processing people to processing ideas. Language, once perceived as solely a means of human communication, soon becomes a mediator and regulator of behavior as well. The language of education not only controls and instructs, it also monopolizes the greater part of a school day. Consequently, the child adjusts by reducing his total response pattern to those terse replies which give him access to the next educational task. Learning now proceeds vicariously, through the economy of the textbook, combined with the synthesizing skills of his teacher. Teachers and students view academic achievement as exclusive to an educational progression where competency in one setting ensures transition to the next. "To get through" becomes the major goal of the child, while "to get him through" becomes the unspoken objective of his teacher.

The elementary school teacher is the first and possibly the last of the panoply of educational personnel given the opportunity to view and treat the child as an entire human entity. Other specialists in the school community tend to address their skills to that portion of each child determined as within their domains. While recent trends in counselor education reflect concerns for the learning process through the vehicle of behavior modification, personal and social development are historically defined as the only purview of the counselor. Basic psychomotor skills are concurrently developed by the physical education teacher, and exposure to the realm of esthetics becomes the responsibility of the art and music teachers. It is not surprising that the child views himself as a fragmented entity upon which specialists operate . . . for those specialists rarely remain on the scene long enough to establish with each other the health of the total organism that is the child. It is doubly tragic if the elementary teacher also sees that child as a vessel into which to pour some subject matter content so as to move him on to the next teacher "processor."

Because most children would rather please than displease the adults who are perceived as in authority, they appear to accept the digested experience relayed to them by teachers. Yet for a time, their out-of-school behaviors continue to be in direct contrast to the highly structured classroom they have just entered. Great joy and release are observed in the play of primary school youngsters, who cling to the exercise of options in adult modeling they had enjoyed in preschool years.

The performance of a task in silence does not preclude the presence of an internal dialogue the child is having with himself. That this dialogue takes as long as two to four years to erupt in either challenge or conformity is a tribute to his faith that the adults who surround him will let him show them who he is and what he can do. Certainly they will reveal a master plan which responds to a multitude of questions about himself: What am I like? How am I changing? What will I be like? Are there others in the world like me . . . and what do they do when they grow up? What do I need to know to do what I *think* I want to do? What does school have to do with anything but more school?

Because these questions are tentative and diffuse in the child's preconscious, they are rarely asked. For most children, it is easier to agree with the proposition that an accumulation of facts will, in themselves, provide the answers. For others, whose rejection of school mores has been earlier identified by the teacher as either emotional immaturity or underachievement, the emergence of aggressive or withdrawn behavior is one of the first of many symptoms of alienation.

What promise does career education hold as an approach to teaching basic skills? And can it begin, as its proponents believe, to answer those unspoken questions every young child asks himself?

Career education is not just a device for using the classroom to attain knowledge and skills useful in the workplace, nor the means to develop the attitude of a productive and obedient worker. It has a reciprocal contribution to make to the objectives and content of academic education. Career education is not a subject matter to be added to the curriculum. It is best defined as a teaching methodology which, as it departs from the single criterion of content mastery, provides a new motivation for learning. It is an approach which extends and returns the abstract to the concrete through a cyclical engagement immediately applying and testing needed skills in a practicable and worldly context. At the same time, it provides the child a vastly peopled landscape from which to draw a multitude of mirror images of himself as he might someday be.

Ironically, traditional education is more correctly described as an imposition of occupational choice than is career education. What could be more specific than the presentation of only two alternatives for a child's future identity? He must choose, at that moment when these alternatives are offered in the primary grades, to be like — or different from — the educated professionals around him. In effect, he elects to be either a professional or a second-class citizen . . . and this election can and does deeply influence the rest of his life.

As a humanistic approach, career education challenges the reduction of a child's early models to a handful of educators. It states that the function of the elementary school should not be to mold children into replicas of its own personnel. On the contrary, that function should be to broaden their contact with people in the world — to actually delay fixation upon a single future identity until all possible future roles have been investigated. Since it is inconceivable that any child will remain mute in the face of his current and consuming desires and interests, his tentative career choices must be heard, encouraged, and fostered through curriculum designed to explore them. The philosophy is clear and attractive. The problem is getting from here to there.

Decisions as to how to relate academic areas to future applications in the world of work will probably be made through extensive testing of the efficacy of all these approaches on a broad enough sample of elementary school children to warrant conclusions supporting action at local agency levels. Elementary school teachers who are known practitioners of career awareness approaches within their own classrooms must immediately be tapped and recognized as models for each investigation. If enthusiasm and creativity are to be maintained within these individual teachers, district and state education department leadership and coordination should be evident in both the experimental and implementation stages of career education.

Many states have effectively recognized and pinpointed exemplary teaching practices through state or regional conferences with a career education theme. In this way, individual schools, personnel, and districts have been able to share their ideas with their professional colleagues. The germ of in-service growth and development proceeds from these and other ways of bringing the educational community together under one roof; but continuing societal support for educational programs can only come through the school-community linkage which will be discussed in the next chapter.

Suggestions for Further Reading

"An Environmental and Career Oriented Science Curriculum."
    Write: William A. Dwyer, Superintendent
            Blue Ridge Regional Technical School
            Canton, Massachusetts

Bruner, Jerome S. "Some Theorems on Instruction (Illustrated, with Reference to Mathematics)." *Theories of Learning and Instruction.* Edited by Ernest R. Hilgard. Chicago: University of Chicago Press, 1964.

Dwyer, J. *Teaching Children through Natural Mathematics.* New York: Parker Publishing Co., 1970.

Kratwohl, David R. "Stating Objectives Appropriately for Program, for Curriculum, and for Instructional Materials Development." *Journal of Teacher Education* 16 (March 1965):83–92.

Moss, Jerome. "The Prevocational Effectiveness of Industrial Arts." *Vocational Guidance Quarterly* 17:1 (September 1968):21–26.

O'Hara, Robert P. "The Roots of Career." *The Elementary School Journal* 5 (February 1962):277–80.

Phillips, Murray G. "Learning Materials and Their Implementation." *Review of Education Research* 36:3 (June 1966):373–79.

Tennyson, W. W.; and Monnens, L. R. "The World through Elementary Readers." *Vocational Guidance Quarterly* 12 (1963): 85–88.

Tiedt, Sidney W.; and Tiedt, Eric. *Elementary Teacher's Complete Ideas Handbook.* Englewood Cliffs, New Jersey: Prentice-Hall, Inc., 1965.

Tyler, L. E. "The Development of Vocational Interests: The Origin of Likes and Dislikes in Ten Year Old Children." *Journal of Genetic Psychology* 86 (1955):33–44.

————. "The Report of Interests and Abilities and Reputation among First Grade Children." *Educational and Psychological Measurement* 11 (1951):255–64.

3

Career Development in the Elementary School

What do we really know about career development? Will emphasizing this phase of career education during the elementary school years force students to make premature decisions on what kinds of work they will want to do later in life? Can the elementary school teacher pinpoint a child's aptitudes, abilities, and proclivities to such a degree that the teacher can guide and even facilitate the youngster's development toward a specific career? These and other questions may rightly be asked by parents and schoolteachers alike. And if the elementary school adopts a career education program, these parents and teachers might also ask: Which aspects of career development should begin in the elementary school? Which should be avoided? We shall endeavor to answer these and other questions in this chapter.

In chapter 1 we identified the career development component as one of five major parts of career education — but career development differs from the others to the degree that it encompasses the others to some extent. Indeed, it could be considered the primary goal of all career education because our ultimate objective is to help individuals develop careers for themselves, to help them understand that work can be possible, meaningful, and satisfying to each of them.

It is necessary to carefully delimit the role of career development as a goal of career education in the elementary school. In brief, by completion of elementary school, the student should have acquired the following: (1) a general awareness of the nature of the world of work, (2) a general awareness of work values as a set of possible reasons why people work, (3) a set of work values that will lead each student to achieve a positive self-concept as one who will someday be a worker, and (4) a view of the world of work from a personalized frame of reference, resulting in tentative aspirations regarding the kind of work he may someday choose to follow. The goals do *not* include anyone's urging on any elementary school student a firm commitment to any specific career goal.

In this chapter we shall attempt to clarify the various shadings of the career development process as it occurs for elementary school children and to illustrate that process by describing more comprehensive career development programs than the fragmented practices in support of the components that were discussed in earlier chapters. Clarification is important as the very basis for understanding and planning specific program activities and for making sure that selected activities are firmly grounded in theory and reason.

To avoid confusion, let us also clarify our terminology by defining the three following aspects of career development:

(1) "Career development" is a goal of career education.

(2) The "career development process" refers to the dynamics of change within the individual as he moves toward career development.

(3) "Career development programs" are the specific methods and procedures used to facilitate the career development process.

Thus career development programs constitute one component of career education, whereas all five components are part of the career development process and contribute to career development. All of the examples in other chapters can be considered parts of the career development process.

Our primary objective here — to discuss the career development process as it is expected to occur in the elementary school — will be done within the framework of human growth and development so that elementary school educators can readily see relationships between this part of career education and the basic principles already familiar to most of them.

The Career Development Process as Part
of Human Growth and Development

Most elementary school teachers have been exposed to a great amount of literature in the field of human growth and development. To the extent that these teachers have effectively mastered the substance of this field, they already know much about career development — e.g., that career development is a normal and expected part of human development for most individuals. As with other aspects of human growth and development, career development is not dependent upon any external force or program for its occurrence. Rather, it represents a personal growth pattern that can normally be expected to occur, in some way and to some degree, for most individuals in our society.

Whether career development is a proper concern of the elementary school will not be debated here . . . for career development is an ongoing process in some manner and degree for most elementary school students. The degree to which elementary schools have been responsible for influencing this development — together with many other aspects of human growth — is the foremost topic of concern.

Certain basic truths regarding human development apply, whether they be in physical, emotional, intellectual, social, or career growth. Each of these truths holds action implications for those dedicated to the operation of programs designed to assist individuals toward optimal development in any of these areas. These truths must be kept clearly in mind by elementary school educators who seek to devise and implement programs of career development. The six following developmental features apply: maturation of the individual, heredity and environment, intellectual development, intervention strategies, remedial assistance, and deprivations that can retard or impede development.

• *Development occurs over the lifetime of an individual and can be described in maturational terms ranging from immaturity in the early years to full maturity in the adult years.* The maturational process cannot be substantially shortened by any known intervention strategy, despite the socially desirable implications of such a concept. We do not expect to witness full vocational maturity by any elementary school student, nor do we expect the student to attain such maturity by the end of elementary school. It would be as fruitless to set a goal of vocational maturity for the elementary school student as it would be to set a goal of physical maturity.

That we are always dealing with some degree of vocational immaturity in working with elementary school students makes vocational development procedures at this level no less important than at any other stage in life. Indeed, it makes them more important at this point than later in life, when basic parameters have already been established and are influencing the individual. If the school does not participate in the career development process, the process will nevertheless continue, but it will be less efficient and more subject to pure chance and to undesirable environmental influences.

As in other aspects of human development, traumatic changes at a certain stage in life may call for rather drastic reappraisal by the individual of those particular dynamics of his career development. Just as traumatic emotional experiences may cause adults to alter their total pattern of emotional development, so may the disappearance of opportunities to engage in a chosen occupation cause them to alter the pattern of their career development. In both instances, however, the early childhood experiences which characterize such development can make it either harder or easier for the person to make developmental adjustments needed in later life.

The total pattern of career development, as in the total pattern of human development, is expected to occur throughout one's lifetime. In the case of career development, this is clearly seen in the increasing numbers of retired workers who, after they retire, embark on what is a new career for them. Career development is truly a part of living itself, not something that ends at a particular point in time in the life of the individual.

In a maturational sense, vocational development differs from other forms of human development in that the process can be repeated more than once in the life of an individual. This is particularly true for the adult worker who, having seen a former occupation disappear because of technological change, must again go through the entire process of occupational choice, preparation, and implementation.

• *Individual development is influenced by heredity and by environmental factors.* Major environmental factors affecting development include those of a physiological, psychological, sociological, educational, and economic nature. These kinds of factors, as they affect human growth and development, are subject to strategies of program intervention which, if carried out effectively by the home or school, can facilitate individual development. These fundamental truths of human development have many applications for career development.

Too many people for too many years have regarded career development from the perspective of an "accident" theory; they seemed content to operate as though "whatever will be will be." Systematic, planned programs, designed to facilitate physical, social, and intellectual development, have long been the prime inputs to the elementary school curricula . . . and there is no valid reason why the elementary school should not assume equal responsibility for positive intervention strategies designed to assist in career development.

Over the years, many elementary school teachers have influenced career development without consciously being aware that they did. An examination of the content in the elementary school reading books adds credence to this theory. Professional occupations are extolled, while skilled crafts and clerical occupations are barely touched upon (in comparison to the large numbers of people actually working in such occupations).

A study completed a few years ago found wide discrepancies between the frequency with which various occupations were mentioned in school readers and the frequency with which those occupations actually exist in the world of work. More recent research has pointed up the limited world shown to young girls through textbooks replete with stereotyped, feminine roles — nurse, schoolteacher, secretary, typist, housewife. If the elementary school has in truth been an unconscious contributor to the false notion that a college degree is the best and perhaps only route to occupational success, or that women are limited to a few service jobs, it can surely be a positive contributor to a more accurate and realistic picture of the actual world of work. Several studies have demonstrated a relative lack of frequency with which students make reasoned occupational choices before they enter school, possibly due in part to the relative lack of attention some pay to positive career development intervention strategies while the child is in the elementary school.

• *Career education assumes that if positive assistance can be given students in career development, intellectual development will be enhanced.* With the increasingly close relationships existing between education and work in the emerging postindustrial society, the above assumption appears to be gaining in credibility, though its validity has always existed. Because excessive deprivation in any single facet of human development can retard optimal development in all other facets (as will be discussed in more detail later), optimal human development programs should be comprehensive and complementary in nature and not limited to any single facet. We find that the basic principle of human growth and development forms a significant part of the rationale for career development activities in the elementary school, particularly in the relationship between career development and intellectual development.

No one who does not understand an economy which provides material support and labor markets which are the arbiters of productivity and achievement can understand the world in which he lives and the society of which he is a part. Emotional stability depends upon feelings of self-worth, and self-worth in turn upon productivity and achievement; even physical development is dependent upon emotional well-being. Elementary school teachers who place high priority on the intellectual development of their students can better attain these goals if they pay some attention to the principles of career development in their classroom activities.

• *Individual development can best be facilitated by intervention strategies that are begun in the very early years and are continued at greater and greater levels of sophistication throughout the life-cycle.* Programs designed to operate only at certain points or at certain stages in the life of an individual are sure to have limited effectiveness. This principle has not been wholly recognized in American education through systematically planned career development programs that span human growth and development from childhood through adulthood. Too many parents and educators still assume that occupational choices will be made at some future magical point in time and that until that time appears, neither we nor our students should worry about such matters. (This assumption is diametrically opposed to the well-tested principle of human growth and development stated earlier. It is an assumption that should be universally discarded.)

Children who enter elementary school without having given thought to possible occupational choices are a rarity. These students' parents may have already considered, however fleetingly, occupations for their children and may have, at various times and in various ways, communicated such thoughts and aspirations to their offspring. The topic of future occupational choice is many times raised by relatives who unwittingly give support to preconceived occupational objectives by asking such questions as "Are you going to be a teacher [doctor, nurse, engineer] when you grow up?" or "Would you like to be an architect [dentist] like your uncle when you get big?" thus reinforcing the concept that a college education is the only path to an ideal career.

Since most elementary school students are in some way giving thought to occupational choices, the elementary school should seek to further the students' career development with a series of planned intervention strategies that would occur throughout the elementary school years. Without pressing children into permanent, premature choices, teachers and guidance counselors can familiarize themselves with situations wherein parents try to bind the child to an early tentative choice ("But you said you wanted to be a doctor, and we have let all our friends know about it. How can you let us down now by choosing to be a —?"). The child will probably change his mind innumerable times, but tentative choice has two advantages: (1) the goal provides motivation, and (2) decision-making skills are learned.

• *Intervention strategies designed to assist in normal maturational stages of human development are more likely to succeed than those designed to provide remedial assistance to individuals whose development has been damaged or retarded.* Again, we find in this basic principle of human growth and development an essential part of the rationale for career education in general and career development in particular beginning in the elementary school.

A wide variety of federal manpower programs in the last decade have been designed to aid those youth and adults who are out of school, out of skills, out of jobs, and out of home. Seemingly massive efforts have been mounted to help such persons acquire personally meaningful sets of work values, marketable job skills, and actual employment. Many individuals have been helped to better employment and higher income, but the impact on the total problem has been minimal. Only a small portion of this pool of unemployed persons with no readily marketable job skills can be accommodated in such programs. The remedial effort is necessary but can offer no long-run solution. Just as crime prevention cannot be accomplished simply by placing criminals in prison, successful career development cannot be accomplished simply by mounting remedial manpower programs for those out-of-school youths and adults who are experiencing difficulties in finding and holding jobs. In the long run, career development must be attacked on a longitudinal, developmental basis beginning in the home and in the elementary school.

• *Economic, social, physical, educational, or psychological deprivations can serve to retard or impede optimal individual career development.* Because those who suffer from such deprivation will require special and intensive assistance, there can be no model career development program universally appropriate for all children. The problems of career development for the socioeconomically disadvantaged are huge and not yet well understood. However, we know enough to realize that special programs of career development must be devised and implemented for this portion of our total school population. Unless this is done, the gap between poverty and affluence — as expressed in earnings of employed adults — is likely to widen. Thus in career development, as in all other phases of human growth and development, the goal is not *equality* of opportunity for all children. Rather, what should be sought is *equity* for each child. Problems of equity vs equality are bound to be very great in elementary school career development programs.

For example, a frequent career development practice for the elementary school centers around the study of common occupations in the immediate neighborhood. If that suggestion were followed in some inner city ghetto schools, the "common" occupations might well include that of drug pusher, prostitute, "hustler," and "numbers man," with few of the promising occupations presented to students in more affluent areas.

Another common suggestion for the elementary school is to encourage students to begin their study of the world of work by learning about their parents' occupations. In some situations, the most common occupation might well be that of welfare recipient. In schools serving such students, special efforts may be required, including the "living witness" approach (former students who have done well), the busing of students to places of employment outside the immediate neighborhood, and the "adoption" of the school by a prosperous business or industrial organization under arrangements where workers, on a one-to-one "buddy" basis, seek to help elementary school students acquire a positive view of work and a broader perspective of the real world of work. For these pupils, the added financial cost may well produce big dividends.

Vocational Maturity as Part of Human Maturation

The "mature" individual is one who, in taking responsibility for decisions he makes, is able to answer in a reasoned and knowledgeable fashion the following three questions: "What is important to me?" "What is possible for me?" and "What is probable for me?" Each of these questions is easily translatable to those who ponder the problem of occupational choice. Elementary school children cannot be expected to arrive at anything approaching "mature" answers to any of these three basic questions by the time they complete the sixth grade. However, this does not mean that significant positive contributions cannot be made during the elementary school years toward helping students begin to formulate answers to these questions.

The first question — What is important to me? — involves work values when one is considering vocational maturity. The next portion of this chapter is devoted to a consideration of work values as part of human values. Here it is important to point out that we are dealing with the basic problems of why people work . . . in the expectation that the child will see himself in a positive light as a future worker. Work can and should be pictured to elementary school children from at least two perspectives. First, these pupils should be made generally aware of the necessity for work, in some form, for economic survival. The necessity of work for societal survival can and should be pictured as quite independent of the desirability of work for individuals in that society.

Unless work is performed, society disintegrates. Some people must work to provide us with food and shelter, and to teach each new generation what has been learned in the past. Technology may reduce the proportion of the population which must work to enabled society to survive, or it may reduce the proportion of time we must each spend in work. Already it has reduced the amount of physical effort which must be expended in work. But no conceivable technology can remove the necessity of work for a substantial proportion of society for a substantial portion of adult life. No matter how sophisticated our machines become, someone must design them, produce them, and repair them. The more sophisticated our society becomes, the more it needs capable workers to enable it to survive.

Second, it is less apparent, but equally true that man needs work if he is to survive. Everyone is familiar with the person who retires from work without having prepared for retirement, and quickly dies or lapses into senility. Clearly, for such individuals work is essential to health and survival. We do not understand fully why this is so. It may be that work is our best means of expressing our feelings of self-worth or of associating with our fellowmen. Regardless of the reason, however, it seems clear that for most people, work is necessary for individual welfare and survival.

The ways in which economic rewards, benefits, and handicaps are associated with specific occupations can and should be pictured in relation to the way in which work operates as an influence on and of the economy. Basic understandings of work from this economic viewpoint can help pupils move toward vocational maturity. In a total program of career development, work as a generic concept must also be understood from a sociological point of view. It is both unfair and unrealistic to emphasize the societal worth and dignity of all honest work unless simultaneous attention is given to the varying degrees of worth our society has afforded various occupations, and the dynamics by which such differential worth is assigned.

From a psychological point of view, work must be seen in terms of interests, aptitudes, skills, and values that are held or may be developed by the individual. While elementary school students can and do consider these topics in terms of possible occupational choices, their limited aptitudinal and vocational skills development limits the degree of personal relevance of these considerations. This in itself makes occupational awareness no less important in helping the pupil think and learn about himself.

The second question — What is possible for me? — is closely related to a psychological view of work itself. Again, vocational immaturity is expected when elementary school students ask themselves this question. We know that differential vocational aptitudes are not highly developed during the elementary school years, and that our ability to measure those that are present in elementary school students is extremely limited. Yet there is no classroom in which abundant opportunities do not exist for demonstrating the concept of differential aptitudes to students. Some students are better at one kind of task and some at others. As all students observe these differences, they are sure to begin to ask themselves where their highest aptitudes are located, what they are able to do best, and what tasks they seem to be relatively unable to accomplish in a successful manner. As they do so, they are moving toward vocational maturity. At this stage particularly, the teacher must be careful not to place high value only on those aptitudes which are useful in school-type learning.

The third question — What is probable for me? — can be answered only through a clear and comprehensive view of the nature of the occupational society at a particular point in time. With the current rapidity of change existing in that society, there is really no good way that today's elementary school student can come up with firm answers to this question that will still be valid when he actually enters the labor market. This in no way means that it is futile or foolish to teach elementary school children something of the basic nature of the occupational society as it exists today. Despite the rapid changes occurring, the occupational world of the near and distant future will be more like than unlike that of today. Students can certainly be exposed to concepts of the great size of the occupational society, the major kinds of occupational families that now exist, the concept of specialization that is present in all broad occupational families, and the concept of occupational change itself. It is here that the fifteen broad career clusters[1] — into which the U.S. Office of Education has seen fit to subsume most of the occupational world — can provide a useful and manageable framework for increased awareness. To become aware of the significance of the question and the fact that it will have to be continually reassessed is in itself helpful in development of vocational maturity among elementary school students.

Though vocational immaturity will characterize the elementary school years, beginning steps in the career development process can help students make significant strides toward vocational maturity by the time they reach junior high school.

---

[1] These clusters are listed in *Career Education: What It Is and How to Do It*, p. 63.

Work Values as Part of Human Values

If elementary school teachers are to help their students become aware of and develop a personally meaningful set of work values, it is essential that these teachers themselves have a clear understanding of the changing nature of those work values, the implications such changes hold for ways in which "work" itself is defined, and the equally important implications for ways in which the word "career" is defined.

Just as career development can be perceived as part of human development, so can work values be pictured as part of one's system of human values. Human values, including work values, begin to develop very early in life — even before elementary school. They are heavily influenced by the value systems of the particular society in which one resides, and are especially susceptible to the influence of values held by one's family, associates, and peers. There is good evidence to indicate that human values, including work values, are heavily influenced by early childhood experiences, can be sharply altered by the school as an instrument of the broader society, and are susceptible to a certain amount of change throughout life, due largely to the social environment in which the individual lives.

In general, it is through such values that an individual finds meaning, direction, and purpose in his life. It is through his work values that an individual finds, or fails to find, meaning, purpose, and direction in both the concept of work and in the particular work that he does. Thus work values are of major importance in individual career development. Our schools, as instruments of society, have always been in the business of imparting certain value sytems to youth, of helping youth develop and find personally meaningful value systems for themselves and, typically, of trying to accomplish both of these purposes simultaneously. Career education asks that work values be incorporated along with other value systems now being taught in our schools.

Work values, like the nature of work itself, are undergoing rapid societal changes. The work values of many youth today are different from those of their teachers or other adults with whom they associate. If we are to be successful in helping youths understand and accept some of the values of a work-oriented society, we cannot hope to do so by ignoring or undermining the values they have developed for themselves. An adult committed to the values, "If at first you don't succeed, try, try again!" may feel that youth prefer the value, "If at *once* you don't succeed, forget the whole thing!" The adult may be convinced that he is right and the youth is wrong, but this conviction is not likely to be a positive force in the development of that youth's work value system.

If there were a different work ethic for each stage of society, its nature would be simple to describe and understand. One could conceive of a subsistence society, without buying, selling, or bartering, in which there was no survival without producing one's own food and shelter. Work would be clearly necessary for survival, and the nonworker would be immediately perceived as a burden upon the worker. Throughout most of its history, the world has approached that model, and much of it still does; but it has never been an exact description.

Weber, in his book on the Protestant ethic vs the capitalistic spirit, argued that some of the theological concepts of Protestantism aided the development of a work ethic necessary to the emergence of capitalism in its early stages. The precapitalist work ethic had admonished: "Produce what you consume with a little extra for kings and priests." The emergence of capitalism required that significant numbers of people produce more than they consume and invest those savings in capital equipment to increase human productivity. Previous religious doctrine had argued that one should accept his place in the society and economy as the will of God for him. Now just as Luther argued that every man could be his own priest, approaching God directly without an intermediary, Calvinism offered a rationale for the pursuit of material wealth. Salvation came by the grace of God who chose to save whom He would, regardless of individual effort.

But the elect of God had a duty to accumulate wealth in order to demonstrate his election, yet was prohibited from ostentatious enjoyment of wealth — a perfect recipe for capital accumulation. Work, be frugal, save, and invest . . . these were the proper criteria for the work ethic of the capitalist. He probably preferred that his workers retain the old, rather than grasp the new work ethic. However, the "get ahead" spirit soon replaced the acceptance of the status quo for the worker too. If he could not become a capitalist himself, he could unite with his fellows to demand a larger share of the joint product of his work and his employer's machines.

Hard work and frugality was an appropriate work ethic for an infant capitalism, but a mature model supplied machines to perform much of the physical work, and nonfrugal consumers were necessary to keep the wheels turning. A postindustrial work ethic would downgrade frugality, relegate physical efforts to machines, and emphasize the human services and intellectual skills not easily automated. Given growing affluence, many can afford to serve without financial reward. In a fully post-industrial society, the work ethic might become a service ethic, but achievement and productivity would still be both a societal and individual necessity.

The world in which we live combines elements of all stages, and no such simple work ethic is possible. It is currently fashionable to proclaim that for many persons in today's society, the classical "Protestant work ethic" is dead. While there is much truth in the allegation, the formulation is too oversimplified to be helpful. In the first place, few seem to be exactly sure what the term "classical Protestant work ethic" really means. In the second place, the concept of work values, in its most basic form, has existed for as long as civilization itself so that, to the extent that the Protestant work ethic included some of these basic values, it must surely not be altogether dead. In the third place, to simply recognize that the variety of work values held by different members of society is increasing is not at all equivalent to saying that any single form is "dead." We need to look at the whole concept of work values much more carefully.

In a preliminary attempt to present work values in a fashion for rational discussion, we have prepared three lists which are shown in tabular form below. Each is intended to picture the values of a work-oriented society from a different perspective. While far from perfect in their arrangement, these three different lists of possible expressions of work values can serve as a basis for thought on the subject. List 1 is intended, insofar as possible, to illustrate those work values that were most commonly held during the time when the work force had primarily an agrarian base.

The old hymn, "Work for the Night is Coming," had practical as well as spiritual meaning for the early settlers of the nation. It was a period when, in comparison to today, there were relatively few "bosses" and where the concept of "middle-management" was even more rare.

List 1	*List 2*	*List 3*
Those who work can eat; those who won't work can't eat.	Those who can't work will be fed.	Those who can't or won't work will be fed.
All honest work has worth and dignity.	Work is a means of gaining societal rewards.	Work is a way of making societal contributions.
Work is essential to individual salvation; to loaf is sinful.	Man is best known through his accomplishments.	Man is best known through service to others.
A task well done is its own reward. A task worth doing is worth doing well.	An honest day's work for an honest day's pay.	All workers need and are needed by other workers.
Hard work brings success.	Pride in one's self comes from recognition by the boss or by fellow workers.	Workers should help one another.
A job worth starting is worth finishing. A worker should do his best at all times.	Most workers have bosses whose directions must be followed.	All workers should get personal satisfaction from their work.
Pride in one's self comes from pride in one's work.	A worker should produce at a quality level neither below nor above that set by his boss or customer.	A meaningless task is dehumanizing.
A penny saved in a penny earned.	Buy now to keep unemployment from increasing.	Buy now before prices go higher.

The individual worker had indeed a great amount of responsibility. He generally knew what his job was and why he was doing it, and was convinced of the importance of doing it.

List 2 is intended to be somewhat indicative of work values that were commonly held during the industrial period of our occupational society (roughly 1860–1950). This was a period where productivity and output were universally valued, where the concept of large industries flourished and were encouraged, where mass production was converted from a theory into a practical reality of the world of work, and where the principles of labor-management negotiations were fashioned and put into practice. The manufacture of goods produced by workers in a factory and distributed in a worldwide market to persons not involved in their production was given highest priority. It was the age of the "industrial giant" and the era when America emerged as the leading industrial producer in the world.

List 3 is meant to be indicative of work values that might be more meaningful to those who work in a service-oriented society. For the last twenty years we have devoted more effort to producing services than goods. With about 85 million people now working in this country, well over 50 million are involved in the production of services, with fewer than 35 million involved in the direct production of goods of any kind. Services include sales, distribution and repair, education, government, finance, recreation, and many other activities.

It would be a very simple matter if each of the above three lists could be said to represent a straightforward and delimited version of work values as they existed in these three periods of our occupational society. However, this is obviously not the case. For example, the phrase "Those who can't work will be fed" was an essential part of the early Protestant work ethic; the phrase "Work is essential to societal survival" has been true for many civilizations over many hundreds of years; and the phrase "Work is a means of gaining societal rewards" is one that even the most "far out" members of today's youth would not strongly argue against.

Thus, rather than a number of discrete sets of work values that were appropriate at various times in our history, we see instead a tremendous mixing of work values from all three of the lists. The phrase "values of a work-oriented society" increasingly takes on a variety of meanings with any one individual's views different from anothers. In general sense, the magnitude of the problem can perhaps best be seen if we recognize that as a nation, we are predominantly involved now in the production of services. Where "productivity" is the goal, work values such as in List 2 appear most appropriate, whereas if "service" is the goal, then those in List 3 might be more compatible for a given worker. The net result is that there is no single set of work values that could be given teachers to transmit to students under an assumption that this is the set we hope all pupils will adopt for themselves.

It is especially important to recognize that employers are likely to expect their employees to possess work values which emphasize productivity. Customers expect sound products and good service from the businessmen and tradesmen with whom they deal. Each individual must build his own set of work values; but the school will have failed if it does not teach each individual that each part of society rewards work values differently. A commune may expel a person who saves the pay he has earned, while a bank may promote him for this same activity. A high output of work may earn praise from a foreman but draw censure from fellow workers.

The student who builds work values which are not accepted by employers can expect to have difficulty in securing and retaining employment. The student who builds work values which are not accepted by consumers will have difficulty in succeeding as a businessman. The student who strives hard for promotion in employment may lose some of his friends.

It would be both unwise and unfair to attempt to impose a productivity-based set of work values on those for whom it does not appear to hold promise of personal meaning. Many other sets of reasons for working exist, each of which can provide personal satisfaction to some members of the occupational society. Such reasons include, but are not limited to factors related to standard of living, fringe benefits, security, surroundings, associates, self-image and self-respect, a desire to be of service, or simply the need to get away from home or to avoid boredom. There is no reason to criticize individuals who build viable work values on such factors. On the contrary, there is every reason to allow individuals to learn of their basic nature and to decide for themselves the extent to which they should be embraced.

As we move further into the postindustrial period, with its emphasis on services and the processing and dissemination of information, the formulation of sets of work values deeply rooted in a desire to be of service to one's fellow human beings becomes increasingly appropriate for ever larger numbers of people. Eventually it may become the most appropriate system of work values for the majority of people.

The Meaning of Career

The term "career" can be defined as the sum total of work undertaken by an individual during his lifetime. It can thus be easily differentiated from the term "career development process," which refers to the total constellation of psychological, sociological, educational, physical, economic, and chance factors that combine to shape the "career" followed by any given individual.

Thus the true meaning of the word "career" is seen as directly dependent upon the meaning one attaches to the word "work." In the agrarian society, "work," broadly defined, was operationally the sum total of activities by which an individual attempted to obtain the necessities of life for himself and his family. In our society, "work" may include activities for which no financial rewards are forthcoming, as well as activities for which one is paid in money, goods, or other kinds of extrinsic benefits.

An ideal career is made up of a series of work experiences, each of which is more personally satisfying than the one which preceded it. Career development leads to increased vocational maturity, which in turn leads to more personal maturity and personal satisfaction. A job which is adequately satisfying early in a career is many times likely to be dissatisfying later on. This factor is one reason that a person can change jobs several times during an ideal career. With increased career maturity comes a better sense of which work will be of greatest service to one's fellowman and at the same time be of most service to one's self. The sum of these two things is a measure of personal satisfaction from work.

For some people, the ideal career is a series of promotions up an occupational ladder, with each step bringing added responsibilities, pay, and satisfaction. For others, the ideal career will lead to promotion up to a certain level beyond which satisfaction seems to diminish. For still others, the ideal career will require lateral shifts into related occupations, or even into a completely new occupational field which offers promise of greater personal satisfaction.

Not everyone of course has an ideal career. Racial, sex, religious, or age discrimination may interfere with an ideal career. Parental or peer pressures may lead one to embark on a less than ideal career. Lack of money or influential friends may impose at least temporary obstacles. Lack of opportunity or of the ambition, self-confidence, and wisdom to recognize and take advantage of opportunity may be the obstacle. Clearly, if we try to impose the same work values on all students, or hold the college-educated professional up as the only model of the successful person, we will interfere with the development of ideal careers for at least some of our students.

It may be helpful to teachers faced with problems of communicating concepts of "work" and "career" to elementary school students to think of "work" in the sense of meeting one's human needs for feelings of self-worth. The need to feel worthy is a basic human need of all individuals. One cannot feel a sense of self-worth without an assurance of some control over one's environment. As one acquires work values and salable skills, he gains more and more in control over his environment; he is no longer bound to a single job and completely subject to economic forces over which he has no control.

For many middle-class persons, the need for feelings of self-worth is expressed in terms of a need for achievement — the need to *do*, to *accomplish*, to be *successful* in material ways. Others denied opportunities for material success in ways generally accepted as socially legitimate will seek a feeling of self-worth either in nonmaterial ways or by pursuing material wealth in a socially illegitimate fashion. If no self-worth is achievable, something within the individual dies or never finds life. The principle that any person is best known both to himself and to others through his accomplishments or efforts toward accomplishment, material or nonmaterial, is essential to an understanding of the true meaning and role of "work." It is here where "aspiration" and "achievement" are most clearly differentiated from each other. Aspiration and achievement come together in defining a person only when one considers the broader question of one's total system of human values — of what he considers to be important, good, and right.

At one point in social history, "work" was regarded as a "calling" — the source of the term "vocation" — the way in which any individual, irrespective of how menial the tasks he performed, accomplished something that served God. It allegedly involved a work ethic that combined aspiration, aptitude, and achievement in ways that charged each individual with doing his best at all times in order that he might earn for himself an eventual place in Heaven. It is easy to see why it may have been, at that time, a powerful inducement to work and why, for some persons in our present culture, it still serves this function. It is equally obvious that for many persons today, this basic motivation for work no longer holds any significant personal meaning. A much more diverse set of reasons for working now permeates our society.

Yet as the total occupational society becomes more and more service oriented in its basic nature, it is obvious that "career" — defined as the sum total of an individual's efforts to accomplish tasks that will in fact provide benefits in some form to other human beings — becomes increasingly germane. Again, the concepts of "productivity" and "service" come together in thinking about the true meaning of work. That is, there has to be some operational way of distinguishing the word "work" from the word "play" in that some form of productivity, as service to others, is obviously essential for societal survival. Thus the term "career" must be defined more narrowly than simply the sum total of the individual's activities aimed at meeting his own achievement needs. In our view, those leisure-time activities consisting of hobbies or recreation should not be confused with what can correctly be called "work."

In this sense, what may be "work" for one individual may well be a "hobby" for another. That is, we are forced to search here for the reason or set of reasons why the individual is pursuing a particular activity. If the individual is engaging in the activity primarily for his own personal enjoyment, with the need to serve others or gain tangible benefits for himself being of little or no importance, we would not call that activity "work." If on the other hand, that activity is perceived by the individual performing it as providing tangible benefits either to himself and to others or to himself alone, then we would say "he works." In this sense "work" does not have to be necessarily pictured as distasteful to the individual in any way. Just because he likes what he is doing in no way means he is not working. Rather, whether productive activity is called "work" or "play" is more properly determined by the basic motivations that caused the individual to undertake the activity in the first place. It is this set of possible motivations that we collectively call "work values." It should be obvious why we feel that the topic is appropriate to introduce to children during the elementary school years.

Approaches to the Career Development Programs

What does the career development component of career education look like as it operates in the elementary school? What kinds of new and different things is the elementary school teacher being asked to do? How can the elementary school educator be sure that career development goals are not emphasized at the expense of other worthy goals of elementary education? How can the basic understandings of the career development process be translated into specific methods and procedures in the elementary school setting? As a final portion of this chapter, some discussion of various categories of career development experiences seems appropriate.

The basic substantive content involved here consists of: (a) the world of work, (b) work values, and (c) the child as a prospective worker. To the extent that this content has previously been ignored in the elementary school, its acquisition does indeed represent a set of additional learning tasks that the elementary school is being asked to assume. At the outset, it is essential to emphasize once again that the time required for accomplishment of these tasks need not come from the actual time allocated for acquisition of basic academic skills. Rather, the time will be found in that devoted to helping students understand better why they are being asked to learn the basic skills of language arts, mathematics, science, social studies, physical education, art, and music. Thus it is essentially a means of helping "school" make more sense to the student.

At the same time, the goals of career development are, in themselves, significant for the elementary school to embrace. Career development is an important part of human growth and development. The furtherance of human growth and development is a fundamental part of the entire rationale behind elementary education in the United States. Thus attention to career development in the elementary schools does not have to be justified solely in terms of educational motivation. The fact that career development activities can and do serve a motivational function provides a fortuitous way of incorporating its content into the ongoing activities of the elementary school. Even if they were not so naturally convenient, the goals of career development would still be essential for the elementary school to adopt.

There exists only a finite set of basic kinds of career development activities available in the elementary school. The class field trip as an observational activity, the use of class visitors and simulated work experiences are discussed in chapter 4 because of their community, business, industry, and labor involvement. They should be remembered there as contributors to career development. This chapter adds the teaching of career development concepts through direct instruction, helping students develop personal systems of work values . . . each as it relates to the basic goals of career development presented earlier in this chapter.

Teaching Career Development Concepts through Direct Instruction

Some elementary schools, after formulating basic career development concepts with which they wish their students to become acquainted, have set about to develop learning packages of various kinds covering such material. Where this is done, the career development concepts are taught directly, with no systematic attempt to use them to emphasize the acquisition of basic academic skills.

An example of this approach is seen in the Fusion of Applied and Intellectual Skills project developed at the University of Florida. This project represents a systematic approach to helping elementary school students consider work values at the same time they are being exposed to the basic nature of the world of work. In this sense, it combines an affective with a cognitive approach to career development. Each of the 65 units of instruction developed is organized around three elements: input, action, and reflection — with the reflective step becoming the focus for value clarification activities. These are carefully worked out and involve rather extensive in-service teacher education. Preliminary evaluations of this approach appear promising.

Other elementary schools, also using learning packages, have attempted to intersperse career dvelopment learning packages with those used in regular academic instructional areas. It is, as yet, too early to make judgments regarding the ultimate values to be gained from one approach as opposed to another.

Helping Students Develop Personal Systems of Work Values

Whenever and wherever pupils are exposed to information regarding the nature of work, the general occupational structure, or examples of work values, it is inevitable that to some extent their own personal value systems will be affected. The development of a personally meaningful set of work values, which allow the individual to picture himself positively as a potential worker, is one of the major goals of career education in the elementary school. It is too important a matter to be considered as an automatic or incidental happening.

The question of personal work values arises most naturally whenever the student considers the question: "What kind of career would I like to have as an adult?" We have stressed repeatedly our strong feelings that no attempts should be made, during the elementary school years, to force any student to answer such questions in a firm, final, or highly definitive manner. To take such a position in no way means that we are opposed to seeing this kind of question raised with the elementary school student. On the contrary, if it can be raised and discussed in a counseling-like relationship, it can be very helpful in the development of the student's self-concept. That is, when a student indicates the type of occupation he thinks might be appropriate for him, he is in a very real sense expressing a great deal about the kind of person he sees himself as being. It should be intuitively clear to the teacher and be made clear to the student that when he ultimately chooses an occupation, he is not only choosing a job but a whole life-style, including standard of living, residential location, friends, hobbies, etc.

This issue of self-concept can, and undoubtedly will become a part of the teacher-student interaction at various times when career development activities are being carried out. The more serious consideration we are suggesting here, however, is not easily developed or carried out in an appropriate fashion as part of the classroom teaching-learning situation. Rather, it is more appropriately carried out in counseling conversations, conducted either on a small group or an individual basis, between students and the professionally prepared elementary school counselor.

There are two major operational problems involved: The first is that bona fide elementary school counselors still exist in only a very limited number of elementary schools and, even where they are present, the counselor-student ratio is typically so high that it precludes a great deal of either small group or individual counseling. The second is that, of all the elementary school counselors now employed, only a few have been made competent, in the course of their counselor education programs, to consider and deal with the problems of career development in a skillful and meaningful fashion.

These two operational restraints have caused some national figures in the field of career guidance to call for the elemination of elementary school counselors. Our recommendations are quite the opposite. In our opinion, immediate attention should be directed toward both increasing the numbers of elementary school counselors and improving the knowledge, understanding, and competence all elementary school counselors possess in the realm of career education in general and career development in particular. Obviously, there are many important duties of the elementary school counselor in addition to those associated with career education. At the same time, helping elementary school students reflect upon and make beginning, tentative decisions regarding personal work values represents a strong and viable plank in the total effort to make the elementary school counselor a part of the professional staff in elementary schools throughout the nation.

SUGGESTIONS FOR FURTHER READING

Arbuckle, Dugald S. "Occupational Information in the Elementary School." *Vocational Guidance Quarterly* 12 (1963):77–84.

Bailey, J. A. "Career Development Concepts: Significance and Utility." *Personnel and Guidance Journal* 47 (September 1968):24–28.

California State Department of Education. "Career Guidance." A Model for Career Development, kindergarten through adult (December 1971).

Cottingham, Harold F. *Guidance in Elementary Schools.* New York: McKnight and McKnight Co., 1956.

Creason, Frank; and Schilson, Donald L. "Occupational Concerns of Sixth Grade Children." *Vocational Guidance Quarterly* 18:3 (March 1970).

Crites, John O. *Vocational Psychology.* New York: McGraw-Hill Book Company, 1969.

Davis, Donald A.; Hagan, Nellie; and Strouf, Judie. "Occupational Choices of Twelve Year Olds." *Personnel and Guidance Journal* 40:7 (1962):628–29.

Dodson, Anna G. "An Occupational Exploration Program for Inner City Elementary Pupils." *Vocational Guidance Quarterly* 20 (1971):59–60.

Gantty, Walter V. "Occupational Preparation in the Elementary School." *Educational Leadership* 28 (January 1971):359–63.

Goff, William H. "Vocational Guidance in Elementary Schools: A Report of Project P.A.C.E." Paper presented at the American Vocational Association Convention, Cleveland, Ohio, December 6, 1967.

Green, Thomas. *Work, Leisure, and the American School.* New York: Langmans, Green & Co.

Grell, C. A. "How Much Occupational Information in the Elementary School?" *Vocational Guidance Quarterly* 9 (1961):48–55.

Gribbons, W. C.; and Lohnes, P. R. *Emerging Careers.* New York: Teachers College Press, Columbia University, 1968.

Gunn, Beverly. "Children's Conception of Occupational Prestige." *Personnel and Guidance Journal* 42 (1972):558–63.

Hales, Loyde W.; and Fenner, B. "Work Values of 5th, 8th, and 11th Grade Students." *Vocational Guidance Quarterly* 20 (1972): 199–203.

Hammond, James J. "Proposal for Occupational Teams." *Compact* 4 (August 1970): 29–31.

Havighurst, R. J. *Human Development and Education.* New York: Longmans, Green & Co., 1953.

————. "Youth in Exploration and Man Emergent." *Man in a World of Work.* Edited by Henry Borow. Boston: Houghton Mifflin Co., 1964.

Herr, Edwin L. *Review and Synthesis of Foundations for Career Education.* Columbus, Ohio: Center for Vocational and Technical Education, Ohio State University, 1972.

————. "Unifying an Entire System of Education around a Career Development Theme." University Park, Pennsylvania: Penn State University, 1969. Working paper.

Hill, George E.; and Luckey, Eleanor B. *Guidance for Children in Elementary School.* Appleton-Century-Crofts, 1969.

Hoyt, Kenneth B.; Evans, Rupert N.; Mackin, Edward F.; and Mangum, Garth L. *Career Education: What It Is and How to Do It.* Salt Lake City: Olympus Publishing Company, 1972.

Kabach, Goldie R. "Occupational Information for Groups of Elementary School Children." *Vocational Guidance Quarterly* 14:3 (Spring 1966): 163–68.

Leonard, George E. "Career Guidance in the Elementary School." *Elementary School Guidance and Counseling* 6 (1972): 198–201.

Lifton, Walter M. "Vocational Guidance in the Elementary School." *Vocational Guidance Quarterly* 8 (1959): 79–81.

Lockwood, Ozelma; Smith, David B.; and Trezise, Robert. "Four Worlds: An Approach to Vocational Guidance." *Personnel and Guidance Journal* 46:7 (1968): 641–43.

McDaniels, C. "Youth: Too Young to Choose?" *Vocational Guidance Journal* 16 (1968): 242–49.

Norwich, Anthony L. "A Career Development Program in the Chicago Public Schools." *Elementary School Journal* 71 (April 1971): 391–99.

O'Hara, Robert P. "A Theoretical Foundation for the Use of Occupational Information in Guidance." *Personnel and Guidance Journal* 46:7 (1968): 636–40.

Osipow, Samuel H. "Implications for Career Education of Research and Theory on Career Development." Columbus, Ohio: Center for Vocational and Technical Education, Ohio State University, 1972. Paper prepared for the National Conference on Career Education for professors of educational administration.

————. *Theories of Career Development*. New York: Appleton-Century-Crofts, 1968.

Reinherz, Helen; and Griffin, Carol. "The Second Time Around." *The School Counselor* 17 (January 1970):213–18.

Roberts, Nick J. "Establishing a Need for a Vocational Guidance Program at the Elementary and Middle School Level." *Elementary School Guidance and Counseling* 6 (1972):252–57.

Smith, Edward D. "Vocational Aspects of Elementary School Guidance Programs: Objectives and Activities." *Vocational Guidance Quarterly* 18 (1970):273–79.

Super, Donald E.; Stariskevsky, Reuben; Mattin, Norman; and Jordan, Jean-Pierre. *Career Development: Self-Concept Theory*. New York: College Entrance Examination Board, 1963.

Tennyson, W. W.; and Monnens, L. P. "The World of Work through Elementary Readers." *Vocational Guidance Quarterly* 12 (1963): 85–88.

Tiedman, David V.; and O'Hara, Robert P. *Career Development: Choice and Adjustment*. New York: College Entrance Examination Board, 1963.

Tyler, L. E. "The Development of Vocational Interests: The Origin of Likes and Dislikes in Ten Year Old Children." *Journal of Genetic Psychology* 86 (March 1955):33–44.

Weber, Max. *The Protestant Ethic and the Spirit of Capitalism*. New York: Scribner & Sons, 1958.

Wellington, J. A.; and Olechowski, V. "Attitudes toward the World of Work in Elementary School." *Vocational Guidance Quarterly* 14:3 (Spring 1966):160–62.

Whitley, John M.; and Resnikoff, A., Editors. *Perspectives on Vocational Development*. Washington, D.C.: American Personnel and Guidance Association, 1972.

Zaccharia, Joseph S. "Developmental Tasks: Implications for the Goals of Guidance." *Personnel and Guidance Journal* 44:4 (December 1965):372–75.

4

School-
Community-
Labor Market
Linkage

It is paradoxical that as we set out to prepare children and youth to participate in the society, we seek to remove them as far as possible from contact with the real world which constitutes that society. It is hard to conceive of a learning environment less stimulating than a walled classroom inhabited by one teacher and 35 students. It may be an efficient device if the intent is to isolate the student from diverting influences while concentrating on the maximum acquisition of abstract facts. It is inefficient if the objective is understanding the relation of the being able to apply those facts to the world beyond the school walls.

It is in society that people must be communicated with and arithmetic applied, where music is heard and sung and art is seen and enjoyed. In that world are the real examples of social problems that the social studies textbook can at best poorly represent and where the technologies and applications of science can make those studies real. Unfortunately, it takes far more imagination and initiative to marshal those experiences in meaningful ways than to prepare a teaching guide from written material — or apply one someone else has written.

Winning the cooperation of people and institutions of the community and labor market absorbed in their own activities is no simple task, yet there are many ways in which the community and the classroom can be linked. Field trips can be taken for observation of real world activities. Visitors can be brought into the classroom. Children and youth, particularly older ones, can become directly involved in real world experiences, contributing to the solution of environmental and other social problems or gaining work experiences through the cooperation of employers. These experiences can be brought back into the classroom, discussed, simulated, and problems, projects, and lessons can be based upon them.

Even though each labor market and community institution has its own concerns and limited social energy, the number of available institutions is great, and each has its own reasons for interest in the conduct and products of the schools. Private employers have a long-term interest in a high-quality, well-motivated labor force and share a taxpayer's interest in reduced social dependence, combined with a businessman's interest in prosperous consumers. Public agencies are also employers and are conscious of the need for public support. Antipoverty, environmental control, and other special interest agencies are anxious for public understanding of the problems they address. Labor unions lament the failure of youth to be taught and to understand the essential role of employee organizations in an industrial society. Politicians are unlikely to risk alienating potential voters and children of voters. If care is taken to avoid overburdening hospitality which conflicts with primary responsibilities of these institutions, cooperation and participation can be gained if sought with diplomacy and forthrightness.

Individual workers have even more reason to cooperate and participate with the schools in career education activities than institutional representatives. They are the parents, taxpayers, and members of the neighborhood and community who share with the schools an affection for young children. But in addition they are likely to have more time and are less likely called upon for community services than those who are assigned to represent their institutions. They may be also more appropriate as role models because more children are likely to be able to visualize themselves in (and ultimately achieve) those roles than the role of manager, politician, or bureaucrat. An additional value may be increased pride in themselves as mirrored in the faces of their own children and in the children of their co-workers. For the average employee, recognition is often hard to achieve, as the following story illustrates:

> George Watson left his shift at the plant and went directly to the corner tavern. To one who listened he said, ". . . So what if

you've made a great weld of a tough angle bend? No one gives a damn. I once suggested [at a union meeting] that we should have some kind of recognition program like the boys in business do when they sell a million dollars worth of insurance. You know, something like 'George Watson made a great weld this week,' or 'George Watson was working with this apprentice and now the kid is coming along just fine.' — People just laughed at me. 'Sit down George,' someone yelled, 'what the hell do you care? You get good pay.' I thought that was worth smashing someone's nose in. But I didn't. I went out and got drunk. There was nothing I could do." [1]

However, even the most cooperative civic- and youth-minded institution or individual can be "turned off" if not approached appropriately, or if the cooperation they extend is abused. Field trips, classroom visitors, and simulated experience may also be a waste of time and energy and boring to students if not carefully planned with objectives clearly in mind. Therefore, some words of counsel on each type of influence are appropriate here. Examples of each are provided for illustration, though we emphasize that each elementary classroom teacher can and will want to develop new projects or adapt available ones to make them more fitting to the objectives and the settings. As noted earlier, curriculum goals can be undertaken which may pursue a number of objectives simultaneously. Although the following examples have been chosen because they involve the community, employers, labor organizations, and other influences from outside the classroom in the career education process, the objective on behalf of the student may be self-awareness (career development skills), career awareness (work reality directed), academic skill acquisition, or human relations skill acquisition.

THE CLASS FIELD TRIP AS AN OBSERVATIONAL ACTIVITY

Field trips to the world of work outside education can make valuable contributions to the goals of career education in the elementary school. Examples are visits to:

(1) Private businesses and work sites of all kinds

(2) Work places of parents, relatives, and neighbors

(3) Public agencies and services

(4) Local unions

---

[1] *Newsweek,* May 17, 1971, p. 86.

(5) City council and other public meetings

(6) Away-from-work interviews, taped or otherwise, with these and
other workers

However, field trips can also — if not carefully planned and executed —
be almost a complete waste of time. In viewing the possible utility of the
field trip, what does the elementary school teacher have to consider?

First and foremost, it is important that the teacher know exactly why
the field trip is being made. A field trip without a purpose is a purpose-
less activity and has no place in the curriculum. Examples of possible
purposes of class field trips include:

(1) Acquainting students with the general nature of the occupational structure in the specific time and space dimensions of
their own communities

(2) Demonstrating the essentiality of various kinds of work to economic or human progress

(3) Demonstrating the ways in which different kinds of work provide a useful set of personal and societal benefits

(4) Helping students see how workers in various occupations make
use of the basic academic skills taught in the elementary school

(5) Helping students understand the need for cooperation and
teamwork in the production of goods and services

(6) Helping students see and understand that different kinds of
skills and expertise are required for different kinds of work

(7) Helping students understand why both "bosses" and "employees" are essential in the world of work

(8) Helping students see first-hand the variety of settings and environmental conditions in which work is performed

The teacher who expects to accomplish all of these purposes in a
single field trip will be disappointed. The best class field trips are those
that involve a very limited set of objectives that are clearly understood
by the teacher, the pupils, and the business-industrial-community setting
in which the field trip is to be conducted.

Second, it is important that the faculty of an elementary school plan
their field trips in a coordinated way in terms of objectives, frequency,
and sites to be visited. Any field trip is costly to the business-industrial

site to be visited in the sense that if pupils are to really learn, there will be some loss in total productivity during the time of the visit. For all teachers to choose the same business establishment is not wise. A business-industry advisory committee to the elementary school can avoid such an error. If the teacher can tell such a committee exactly what it is hoped the class will gain from a field trip, such an advisory committee can be helpful both in suggesting possible best places to visit and in making actual visitation arrangements. In the absence of such a committee, one staff member in the school can be appointed field trip coordinator to contact employers and determine that they are not being overused and abused.

It is especially important that teachers in a given elementary school coordinate field trips in terms of their basic objectives. To repeat trips with the same objectives for the same students year after year is bound to "turn students off" to some extent. This need not happen, and certainly it should not happen. There are many ways in which the scoping and sequencing of trips can be divided among teachers in a given school. For example, a particular elementary school may seek to acquaint students with the general nature of the world of work in fourth through sixth grades. The U.S. Office of Education has formulated fifteen occupational clusters[2] covering most occupations in the total world of work; others have advocated differing cluster systems — all of which provide useful formats for a general awareness of the occupational world. If the fourth, fifth, and sixth grade teachers each plan to acquaint pupils with five of a total of fifteen career clusters, students can become generally aware of all fifteen by the end of the sixth grade, with no overlap between different grade levels. There may be one outcome that is pursued only by one teacher at one grade level; there may be other outcomes pursued by teachers at all grade levels. But each teacher could contribute to a different emphasis within the same or different settings.

An example of scoping and sequencing cluster exposure can be found in an Iowa exemplary project.[3] These take into account the child's ability to accommodate increasingly wider horizons as he matures. They

---

[2] Kenneth B. Hoyt, et al., *Career Education: What It Is and How to Do It* (Salt Lake City: Olympus Publishing Company, 1972), p. 63.

[3] Taken from the Models for Career Education in Iowa; Elementary. Iowa State University and Iowa Department of Public Instruction, Ames, Iowa.

also find applicability in sequence to the program entry age of the child. For example:

(1) Level I might consist of those occupations that the child has direct contact with during his day, those that directly affect his way of life. These should be visible occupations where something is being made or done that the child can see.

(2) Level II includes occupations that directly affect the child or his family, the occupations again being those the child can visualize as a product or service.

(3) Level III has those occupations that affect him indirectly through his family or community. They would be occurring in settings to which he would not ordinarily have access.

(4) Level IV has those occupations that the student may not be aware of at all. They would typically deal with the more abstract or hidden types of work or product components.

Broken out into categories of self, family or self, family or community, and "unknown," an excursion in the marketing and distribution cluster might appear as:

Self	*Family or Community*
Door-to-door salesman	Auctioneer
Store clerk	Vending machine collector
Billposter	Welding consultant
Deliveryman	Shipping clerk
	Circulation manager
Family or Self	*Unknowns*
Salespeople	Market researcher
Carpet cutter	Advertising manager
Window trimmer	Account executive
Truck driver	Personal shopper
Bank teller	Floor manager

Third, it is highly advisable that the teacher make a "dry run" through the field trip prior to taking the class on the actual trip. If this is done, the teacher will know in advance what the students will be seeing and what activities are planned for them. Personal contact can be established with the key individuals who will be responsible for handling the visit at the work site. The teacher and management should agree on such "ground rules" as how long the students will stay, whether they can interact personally with workers at work stations, the kind of introduction (if any) to be made by officials at the visitation site, whether refreshments will be served, and the numbers of students the business can expect to have visit them. Such a "dry run" will help the visitation site get ready for the students and will also help the teacher ready the class for the work site.

Finally, it is important that the students be instructed (at the school and before the actual visit) as to their behavior and the real objectives of the visit. It is doubtful that any planned objective for a field trip can be accomplished unless the students know what the objective is prior to making the visit. In fact, students can enhance their own career awareness by entering into the planning of field trips. The teacher should also plan some follow-up activities after the visit has been completed.

An alternative to actual visits could be to take small groups of students on a field trip with their being assigned specific tasks to be accomplished and then have them report their findings to the rest of the class. This method has been found by many teachers to be more effective and cheaper. Eventually, all students get to go somewhere — the class has had the advantage of several field trips rather than just one. Parents or paraprofessionals provide transportation in these cases. Tape recorders and cameras can enhance the productivity of the experience. Again, to avoid sites being overused, the business-industry advisory committee, the field trip coordinator in the school, or a career technician who serves an entire district or county can be used to arrange these visits. In the absence of this service, teachers themselves, as discussed in chapter 6, can best work out their system of articulation.

It will be rare indeed if any stated outcome can be accomplished completely at the visitation site. Students will need some time after they return to the classroom to discuss the visit in terms of the differing perceptions they received and what the visit meant to different students. By systematically planning such follow-up activities, the teacher can help correct misimpressions particular students received and, at the same time, reinforce and more effectively maintain the basic concepts surrounding the purpose of the visit.

An example of individual student expeditions which can then be brought back into the classroom for exchange with other students is the practice in a densely populated California city[4] for elementary school children to be "officially late" to school on certain days. They enter a local bus or trolley at peak worker transport time in the early morning and ride to the end of the line and back. During the trip, they interview people on the bus about the work they do and how they use English, social studies, math, or science in the performance of that work. At school, they compare notes on their random sampling and build a chart which tallies the numbers of people in each job category, as well as a consensual "mean" as to the like/dislike reflected by each worker. Thus academic skill acquisition, as well as career awareness, is furthered.

Field trips can also be combined with simulated work experiences while developing human relations skills as well as career awareness. Arizona, the site of one of six U.S. Office of Education school-based models, has launched a statewide effort to introduce career education as the basis for the entire educational process.[5] Children there find themselves the writers and actors, as well as the audience, for a television series called "The Three Rs Plus." The cameras follow students into their communities as they visit workers and return with the students to their classrooms where they merge life skills with basic academic skills and devise new scripts from viewing teachers, communities, and children in other schools.

Teachers can capitalize upon the child's open admiration for physical prowess and poise by asking him to spend a full day observing parent, neighbor, or older sibling at work. Children could record the physical skills they see employed on a prepared form. After reports to their classmates, they could create a wall mural depicting careers calling for:

Fine muscle coordination	Eye-hand dexterity
Large muscle coordination	Long hours at desk or in car
Long hours on feet	Sleeping during daylight hours
Balance and comfort in high,	(night shift)
open spaces	Ability to concentrate despite
Climbing skills	noise and distraction, etc.

[4] Taken from the Career Guidance Development Project, Sonoma County Board of Education, Santa Rosa, California.

[5] Taken from Career Education in Arizona, Arizona State University and Arizona Department of Education, Phoenix, Arizona.

Visitors from the World of Work

It is often more efficient to bring representatives from the world of work into the school than to take students to the work setting itself. Whenever and wherever career education goals are addressing perceptions workers have of themselves and of work — as opposed to the basic nature of the work task itself — it is desirable to use the classroom rather than the work site as the primary learning environment. Several types of class visitors can be considered here:

(1) Community workers and parents can be brought in to serve with teacher groups as participants.

(2) Members of the retired community can be used in classrooms as speakers on careers or satisfying leisure activities.

(3) Members of the working community can be brought in to talk about their jobs and leisure activities.

(4) Members of the community representing alternate life-styles (communal living, welfare recipients, college graduates working with arts and crafts, etc.) can be brought into the classroom to discuss the satisfactions of that life-style.

(5) Parents can come into the classroom with the tools of their trade.

(6) Candidates can be brought in to discuss their political platforms and previous occupations.

(7) Members of the teaching staff can be surveyed as to other jobs they have held or are holding, and can be used as resources.

(8) Each student can spend a day at work with his father, mother, uncle, or neighbor.

(9) Members of local unions can come into the classroom.

(10) Personnel managers can visit to discuss hiring procedures. Video tapes can be made of them interviewing applicants. Students can role-play some techniques.

Many elementary schools have found it valuable to ask parents to come to school for purposes of discussing their occupations with students. The use of parents for such purposes holds many advantages, including:

(1) The spectrum of parental occupations for members of a given class has some relationship to occupations that in fact are most

likely to become available to pupils themselves. There is an element of occupational reality here that cannot be ignored.

(2) For the parent to describe his occupation holds positive potential for enhancing feelings of self-worth on the part of both the parent and the child.

(3) It is often easier to make contacts with the world of work through parents than through strangers in the community.

(4) By involving parents in the career education process, parental understanding of and support for that program will likely be enhanced.

Before embarking on a series of parent visits, students should be clearly aware of the inherent worth and dignity of all who work, that everyone who works is affecting — if not directly helping — some other members of society, and that a variety of reasons exists which lead people to want to work.

The use of parents as representatives of the world of work seems to work best when both parents and class members are given a set of suggested questions or topics to be discussed before the parents arrive. Appropriate questions that parents can be asked to talk about include:

(1) How does your work help other people?

(2) What do you like most about your work?

(3) How did you learn to do your job?

(4) What advice would you give someone who was thinking about doing the kind of work in which you are engaged?

By making both parents and pupils aware of questions such as these, we can often avoid the more direct or potentially embarrassing questions of:

(1) How much money do you make?

(2) What are your chances for advancement?

(3) What is the worst part of your job?

(4) What made you decide to go into this kind of work?

While such questions are essential to consider in the total configuration of the child's career development, they are not appropriate when parents are describing their occupations for members of the class. If the teacher will remember that the goal is to draw out the *positive* aspects of occupations of all parents, most of these inappropriate questions can be avoided.

"Rent a Kid" was the motto created by North Carolina fathers, uncles, mothers, and friends who "adopted" an elementary school youngster and gained an entirely new look at their own jobs as they spent a week together exploring their jobs and workplaces.[6] The community-linked career awareness program has involved the business and parent community to such an extent that parents insist upon submitting to the same interest, aptitude, and attitude assessment inventories which are administered to their children. Moreover, those parents and workers who have free time during the school day are often found reviewing filmstrips, bringing resource materials into the school setting, or becoming absorbed in a class project. The primary purpose is career awareness, but the children are offered exposure to human relations skills as well.

Another useful classroom visitor is the former elementary school student who, after leaving a particular school, went on to complete his education and subsequently attained some success in the world of work. The general approach illustrated by the concept "I came out of this school and made it in the world of work" is a powerful inducement for elementary school students to begin to think about themselves as autonomous young adults. The former pupils most appropriate to use here are generally young people between the ages of 18 and 25 who (if they did not attend this particular elementary school, at least grew up in the neighborhood in which this school is located). With this type of visitor, primary emphasis should be placed on the kinds of experiences the former student encountered between the time he left the elementary school and the present.

Such former students can be very helpful in emphasizing their education preparations, their attempts to enter the labor market, and their probable occupational futures in a positive way. Students listen to them with respect, admiration, and belief. For this reason, it is especially important that former students be carefully briefed by the teacher before they appear in the actual classroom setting. Such briefings should em-

---

[6] Taken from The Apex Project, Wake County Schools, Raleigh, North Carolina.

phasize the goal of giving students an honest, accurate perception of experiences, a minimum exposure to technical aspects of their work, the desirability of avoiding use of language that would confuse pupils, and a willingness to answer questions that pupils raise in ways that avoid to the greatest possible extent the use of direct advice, urging, or persuading.

A third possible type of classroom visitor is the representative from the business-labor-industrial community who can discuss a broad cluster of occupations. Although this type of visitor may be hard to find in small communities, the teacher likely will be able to recruit someone from a neighboring larger city. The goal here is to find an individual capable of discussing, in very broad terms, an entire occupational cluster such as health occupations, transportation, or manufacturing. When one attempts to find a representative from such a broad occupational cluster who is actually employed now, it is inevitable that the occupation in which he is actually employed is considerably more limited than the cluster supposedly under discussion. The only way this approach can work is if the representative is clearly aware of the reasons why he is being asked to meet with the class and has accordingly made considerable preparation for the visit.

In view of the importance of this aspect of career education and the relative infrequency with which qualified members of the actual business-labor-industrial community can be located, many elementary schools will find it rewarding to seek the skills of the elementary school counselor in this assignment. The elementary school counselor who has been exposed in graduate studies to the psychology of occupational choice and career development should be able to discuss broad occupational concepts in a meaningful fashion with elementary school students. When qualified members of the actual business-labor-industrial community can be located as well, a maximum benefit is realized. Where neither is available, the discussion of broad occupational clusters necessarily will fall back on the classroom teacher.

A Maryland school system constructed career "satellites" around a central hub of a kindergarten through twelfth grade school configuration by identifying specific business or industry personnel in each "moon" (career area) who could provide either the work observation or school demonstration appropriate to the age and maturity level of the children.[7]

---

[7] Taken from the Career Satellite Program, Prince Georges County Board of Education, Upper Marlboro, Maryland.

The representatives are within access of each feeder school. Each satellite group plans with the school's multilevel team a sequential program which neither duplicates trips and visits nor conflicts with developmental and classroom learning activities. Satellites are located through the dual efforts of local civic agencies and a school-based teacher with experience in business and industry.

Retired adults in a Baltimore inner-city neighborhood serve as resources to the teachers in the classroom.[8] Women teach boys and girls the craft of weaving, spinning, and quilt making. The slow, painstaking art of glassblowing, ship bottling, and whittling hand-made tools and musical instruments are shared by grandfathers. These oldsters are former bank presidents, carpenters, shipbuilders, dressmakers, nurses, and one-room school principals who — as they give children a sense of history and of unboxed time, along with career awareness and human relations skills — are gaining a new incentive for living.

The rationality of the distribution of career opportunities among various groups can also be tested by selecting appropriate visitors. Maryland teachers who use the "Calling Careers" television series teachers' manual ask students to collect as many comic strip characters as they can find who seem to represent consistent work roles.[9] They discuss how the artist conveys the qualities and life-styles of these people. Teachers encourage students to find exceptions to visual stereotypes and implied sexual or racial role limitations by their citations of people they know who defy them. Students invite and interview representatives of all media to determine the rationale for the newsman's or the artist's seeming "caricatures" of human beings, acquiring in the process career awareness, academic skills, and human relations skills.

Not just the nature of jobs but the usefulness of academic and other learnings can be illustrated by proper choice of visitors. For instance, a physical education teacher might invite people from the community who exemplify psychomotor skills in their work. Their presence is used as motivation for the acquisition of a wide repertoire of physical competencies, while the students also gain career awareness and human relations skills.

---

[8] Taken from the Maryland Career Development Project; Elementary. Division of Guidance and Placement, Baltimore, Maryland.

[9] Taken from the Mid-Hudson Career Development and Information Project, State Education Agency of New York, Albany, New York.

Many speakers from industry are reluctant to speak to groups of children, especially small children, because they feel uncertain as to what to say. A Career Information Center in a California school district gives guidelines to these speakers to alleviate this anxiety.[10] The following list of questions is given them. They are also told to keep their presentation informal and not to talk more than twenty minutes, allowing the remaining time for students to ask questions.

(1) What special interests or skills do you need for your job?

(2) What other occupations can you do with your knowledge and training?

(3) What ways can I get this job — training, college, or experience?

(4) What type of person do you have to be in order to like and be successful at your job?

(5) What are all the different jobs you've had and which have led to the one you have now?

(6) Do you think that your mistakes have helped you to make better decisions?

(7) What types of things (interests) do you like to do, and how did they help you decide what job you wanted?

(8) What school subjects do you use in your work and how?

(9) How has your particular job changed over the past ten or twenty years? What do you think it will be like in another ten years?

(10) How does this job support your way of living in terms of income, knowledge, working hours, and leisure time?

(11) Are your hobbies like or different from your job?

(12) Why is this job important to you? What satisfaction do you get? Do you know of any common factors a person should possess to be successful in the world of work?

Elementary school children in New York State are often the instigators of the most relevant questions chosen for response by local workers who serve on speakers' bureaus, write monographs describing real work options in neighboring counties, and broadcast on local radio stations.[11]

---

[10] Career Guidance Project, *loc. cit.*
[11] Mid-Hudson Career Development and Information Project, *loc. cit.*

They also benefit from their teachers' summer work experiences in local industries where these teachers are exposed to various work functions under the guidance of "advocates." These teachers return to write curriculum which translates their experiences into valid schoolwork concepts and gives added credence to discussion of current and future skills of employability. For the children, the project combines career awareness, academic skill acquisition, and human relations skills.

SIMULATED WORK EXPERIENCE

There is only so much that students can learn about the nature of work through such vicarious experiences as reading, observing, and listening to others. Like learning to swim, learning to work must be experienced in order to become personally meaningful to the student. Increasingly, elementary school children find it difficult to experience work in settings outside the school. Knowing that work values will be developed during the elementary school years, more and more elementary school teachers are attempting to help their students experience work through some kind of simulated activity that takes place largely within the school setting.

The simplest and most traditional approach is to create a series of specified "jobs to do" within the classroom, and assign students to each job on some kind of rotating basis. Such "work tasks" as passing out workbooks, taking roll, directing traffic within the building, supervising playground time, picking up class assignment papers, and keeping the coat closets neat and orderly are examples of kinds of work that are typically assigned elementary students.

Where this approach is used, there is little direct time taken from instructional activities per se. While some elementary teachers have viewed this as an advantage, it in fact represents a potential danger. That is, simply to assign work tasks in no way guarantees that students develop any real concepts regarding the nature of work. They may simply feel that the teacher is taking advantage of them. Thus it is important, if this is the approach to be used, that the teacher take time to make sure that students understand that they are demonstrating, through their actions, such basic work concepts as the social significance of work, the interdependence of workers on one another, the necessity for workers to cooperate with one another, the importance of completing assignments on time, the principle of worker responsibility for carrying out assignments, and the way in which each worker contributes to some broader objective than can be seen from viewing only the specific work tasks assigned to him. The skillful elementary school teacher will find many opportunities to emphasize and reinforce such basic principles again and again during a school year. How frequently they should be emphasized depends upon how often students appear to forget them as they perform (or fail to perform) specific work assignments.

A more sophisticated approach to simulated work experience is the "product outcome" technique oriented around a "company" formed by the students. This approach asks the teacher to help the children think of a product or a service they wish to produce or offer, organize the management-worker system required, assign various students to different roles in the "company," actually "manufacture" the product (using assembly-line techniques), package it in some form, and then make it available either to students within the school or to persons outside the school. Such an approach is not only more authentic but, in addition, allows students to explore the nature of a wide variety of occupations.

Examples of "products" that have been "manufactured" in projects of this nature include puzzles, wall plaques, artificial flower arrangements, note pads, doll clothes, silk screened posters, and games of various sorts. In some cases, special industrial arts equipment, including hammers, saws, drills, and planers, are required. (There are a number of companies now producing such equipment, with a variety of safety devices built in, that come in portable units for use in elementary schools.) In such "companies," students play a wide variety of work roles, including those of both management and labor.

Students on the assembly line may actually experience the boredom and frustration that comes with repetitious tasks. The personnel management staff can actually see how the making of various personnel decisions affects worker morale and plant productivity. All students can recognize the interdependence of one worker on another, the importance of completing assignments on time, the rewards associated with quality production, and the waste that accompanies slipshod work. In some schools, this type of project has been carried to the point where "stock" is sold, with the various "stockholders" receiving dividends on their investment at the end of the project — depending upon the success found in marketing the product. Where several teachers in a single building are using this approach, competing companies may be established that add a still further note of realism to the entire simulation effort.

Many other hands-on activities for elementary school students increase career awareness and sometimes self-awareness, as well as enhancing human relations skills and aiding academic skill acquisition, even though not directly simulating work activities. Children in West Virginia construct "experience" charts of one working adult in their family after taping interviews at home.[12] These charts depict the sequence of career choices that an adult has made through either the free drawings of the child, snapshops from the family album, or a magazine illustration of that activity being done by another adult. The year that the family member was born is noted, as are the dates of subsequent career changes. Children then begin to construct their own charts, noting their current interests and hopes on the dates they occur, adding understanding to both a single career pattern and increasing self-awareness.

A career awareness program built around the stimulus provided by a television series created and shown locally in Memphis permits children to react to broad career clusters of health, transportation, construction, etc., as they are accurately·represented in the local community.[13] Each telelesson guide provides gaming situations, vocabulary development through spelling bees, crossword puzzles, riddles, or mathematic applications derived from the work of familiar adults in the community, thus providing career awareness and academic skills acquisition. Included also is the recognition and use of simple tools in role simulation activities which can be accommodated in the classroom.

In Nebraska,[14] children build a wall mural depicting their "models" for community workers who

Provide food	Teach them new skills
Provide housing	Entertain or amuse them

---

[12] Taken from the Lincoln County Exemplary Program, Hamlin, West Virginia.

[13] Taken from SPAN (Start Planning Ahead Now), Memphis City Schools Exemplary Project, Memphis, Tennessee.

[14] Taken from Project Devise (Developmental Vocational Information and Self-Enhancement), Alliance, Nebraska.

Protect them	Provide for their material wants
Keep and make them well	and needs
Get them from one place	Make them aware of the needs
to another	of others

by using snapshots of people whom the children recognize and who are involved in these roles. The children string "lines" from the snapshots to local addresses or telephone numbers which are taped beneath each photo. A byproduct of the hands-on experience is self-awareness as well as career awareness.

Primary grade teachers attending a Maryland State Education Conference on Career Education were urged to scout the community for the contents of "prop" boxes containing the clothes and tools of parents or other known adults working in broad career areas within the accessible community.[15] Using discarded beer cartons to hold the identifiable costumes, they could secure the assistance of both those workers and the students in filling and decorating each box for role-playing in the classroom. Topping off each box were self-addressed postcards and telephone numbers of each worker the prop boxes represented. These individuals were later used by the children to authenticate their classroom dramatizations.

A multilingual population of elementary school children in New York City are communicating with each other and with the working adults who live around them through the agency of career awareness learning modules published by the *New York Times*, at the request of a Bronx school district's Career Resource Center.[16] Each child is able to respond to adult autobiographies, exercises in the estimation of the worker-personality characteristics requisite in real and local careers, practice in the reading, writing, and vocabulary skills related to success in broad skill areas, questionnaires whose results will be later published in the same modules, and opportunities to express themselves through cartooning, "advertising," poll-taking, poetry, etc. Each "lesson" utilizes all the languages with which the child is familiar while combining career awareness and academic skill acquisition.

---

[15] Adapted from the Maryland State Department of Education's "Calling Careers" instructional television teacher manuals.

[16] Taken from District Seven's Career Resource Center, The Bronx, New York.

After sixth grade Maryland students have visited a nearby hospital's pediatric wing, or an institute for handicapped or disturbed youngsters, they plan with their teacher and the resource people in the feeder junior high school to create four items which will brighten the surroundings of these children.[17] Girls and boys work together in the nearby junior high school's home economics and industrial arts laboratories with their experienced older peers who are already involved in a career studies program. For three hours a week, they work on brightly colored stuffed animals and pillows, wall plaques, yo-yos, blocks, colorful pop-art posters, etc. "Delivery" day is the beginning of a continuing relationship with children less fortunate than they. The project combines self-awareness, career awareness, and human relations skills.

There are two prime difficulties encountered in a project-oriented, work simulation approach in the elementary school. The first is the necessity for equipment and materials to produce the desired products. Given a clear knowledge of the kinds of things that will be available, the good teacher can devise and plan a project that will usually get around this difficulty. The second and more serious difficulty is in devising project activities in which the basic academic skills of reading, communication, social studies, math, science, art, and music can all be increased as a natural part of the project. That is, unless conscious and conscientious attempts are made to avoid this difficulty, it is easy to wind up with a situation where the project appears to be a goal in itself. This is not consistent with those goals of career education related to increasing academic motivation. The teacher must plan the total project in ways that each of the skills is taught at an appropriate time and place at various points in the total project. Here the reader is reminded of those activities in chapter 3 which did not isolate a student activity or project from the context of ongoing learning. It is also valuable to emphasize these activities which relate service to product; e.g., the manufacture of soft toys for infants could be the beginning of a school's adoption of a foundling home nearby.

Sources of Initiative

Undoubtedly hundreds of examples exist across the nation of individual teachers who have reached out to the community, to employers,

---

[17] Department of Mental Hygiene, Maryland State Department of Health, Baltimore, Maryland.

labor organizations, public agencies, and individuals for assistance in bringing the world into the classroom or making of the world a classroom. Whereas, the initiative must ordinarily be the school's responsibility, scores of business firms and, less often, other organizations and individuals have sought out the schools to offer assistance. The school is usually, but not always, the instigator of a visitation program which recognizes workers' needs to receive recognition and variety, even in the humblest of tasks.

Certain companies (e.g., the Corning Glass Works in Medfield, Massachuetts; the American Telephone and Telegraph Company; the Polaroid Corporation; and Xerox, among others) have built-in options of "sliding time" for their employees. These "sleitzits" permit workers to participate as contributors to elementary education programs during school hours by either providing work observation experiences to those children or school demonstrations of their craft or service.

Examples are frequent of the voluntary involvement of business, labor, and industry, offering their services through action methods designed to increase the visibility and importance of school-acquired skills. In candid expressions of self-interest, combined with a real sense of community responsibility, existing industry-education councils are demonstrating more than lip service to career education programs. Among those, the North Carolina Industry-Education Council (an eighty-member group made up of school and community leaders from throughout the state) makes it a practice to visit innovative career education programs nationwide. With the greater share of travel expenses borne by the business community, these individuals return to their home towns with fresh new ideas to adapt or modify for their own educational programs.

The Dallas Chamber of Commerce appointed a fifty-member team of businessmen who contributed more than $125,000 worth of consulting time to the Dallas school system for a school board cost of only $20,000 — the salary of one full-time businessman to staff an ad hoc study on cost effectiveness. Since that time, these and other individuals, rewarded by seeing their recommendations put into practice in a system which had formerly been an unknown to them, are serving as career education resource teams to many local schools. The Skyline Advisory Board to the Dallas schools opened the largest occupational resource plant in the nation recently — where career cluster committees involving more than 220 companies and 231 private citizens have donated more than half a million dollars in time and equipment. School systems in eleven Texas townships are directly involved in this venture, which serves as a theater for continuing education.

Actually, business initiative may be better known than school initiative because the teacher has less reason and less facility for publicity. But since the curriculum itself and the identification of learning opportunities and their integration into the curriculum are an educational responsibility, the primary responsibility resides in the teachers.

Common to school-industry-community linkages, whether supported by federal or local funds — or moved by the will and local resources of the schools or by the community institutions involved — are certain broad goals which seem to exemplify a joint commitment to their young people. They are expressed as follows by spokesmen of school and community:

(1) We will maintain and authenticate the child's positive view of himself as it relates to a diversity of future working roles he might assume.

(2) We will provide experiences which permit the child to observe and react to adults who work in a variety of settings.

(3) We will provide experiences which develop skills in role-playing, drama, reporting, interviewing, listening, looking, touching, manipulating, in order that the child can more accurately approximate the connections between his current interests and the rewards and demands of a career.

(4) We will encourage self-assessment and decision-making skills through work-simulation experiences and projects developed through the vehicle of curriculum.

(5) We will support effective transition from this educational setting to the next by having children forecast the opportunities they will have to test and develop their interests in terms of their increasing capacity.

Another way to implement linkage between community and schools is being carried out in several California State Colleges through a three-week "Bridging the Gap between Industry and Education" course held during three weeks every summer.[18] Counselors, administrators, and teachers receive three units of graduate credit for visitations to fifteen to twenty business and governmental agencies to observe the functions and work settings of those organizations. Objectives are:

(1) To acquaint participants with company or agency operations

(2) To provide participants first-hand observations of various jobs in the company or agency structure

(3) To have participants talk directly with employees about their jobs

(4) To provide participants with relevant information about jobs in local industry which might be useful in counseling students

(5) To acquaint participants with specific skills and qualifications needed in various jobs

(6) To afford participants opportunities to realize some of the problems of local industry and thereby develop more cooperative attitudes toward the world of business

(7) To afford participants opportunities to develop contacts in local industry who might be called upon for further information

Most agencies are provided a list of these objectives, and both class participants and community participants evaluate the extent to which the objectives were achieved.

These are some of the many ways in which the school and community can become linked in a common effort — the making of relevant education through career education. There is a variety of ways in which this link has been accomplished. One obvious way is to have someone research the community and find people representing many different occupations who are willing to talk to youngsters, and then publish the list. There are two obvious problems with this method. One is that teachers tend to call the first person on the list. This person soon becomes overextended and the others on the list are never involved. Another obvious problem is that the material soon becomes outdated and is no longer usable.

Another way to maintain a school-community linkage is to have career fairs where many people representing many different jobs come

---

[18] Career Guidance Development Project, *loc. cit.*

together in an auditorium, and groups of students talk to those they are interested in. With this method there is very little connection between what is happening in school and the information they receive from the community speakers. It is not integrated into the entire curriculum, and that after all is the essence of a comprehensive career education program.

Another major problem is organization. Several counties in California and in other parts of the nation have developed a Career Information Center which, in addition to providing career information to students, keeps an up-to-date file of community resources.[19] A teacher may call one telephone number, and a technician who provides the service can arrange for a speaker to be in the classroom on any date. The technician keeps track of the number of calls to each community resource person and can see that no one person is overworked. The phone can be placed on an automatic answering and coding device, which means that the teacher can call between 5 P.M. and 8 A.M. and leave a recorded message that the technician can carry out during working hours.

Another aspect of this center is that students can talk to the technicians about career information. The technician has available the most current written career information and can discuss this with the student. If the technician is unable to answer some questions, the student can be put on "hold" while the technician calls a person working at that job in the community, and then puts the student and worker in direct communication in a "conference call." Elementary school teachers have used a telephone amplifier during such a call so that the entire class could talk to some worker on his job site.

It is necessary of course to continue to keep an extensive list of community resource people. The communities' service clubs are an excellent resource. Usually these clubs have a vocational guidance committee which is cooperative in getting the names of club members who will act as career counselors. If the center does not have the name of someone who represents an occupation that a teacher wants, then the technician uses the yellow pages of the telephone directory.

RATIONALE FOR COMMUNITY-SCHOOL LIAISON

The need for formal linkages between the school and institutions of the community and the labor market is inherent in the trends of

---

[19] *Ibid.*

modern society. The growing experiential distance between the consuming world of the home and school and the serving and producing community and workplace make it difficult for children to develop a sense of time, of age — past and future. In an "instant culture" trained by the preprocessed data of various media to expect immediate gratification, each generation tends to draw uneasily away from, or be rejected by the voices and examples of the previous one. Committed to the strategy of prolonging childhood in the name of its preservation, educators feel this unease most keenly. The schools surround the young with stimuli and refrain from voicing any value system, while the teacher personifies one value system by omitting references to others.

In too many schools, direct access to the sources of cultural continuity is typically sacrificed to order and mass processing. The child is denied the option of accepting or rejecting a multitude of values he sees or hears professed, and the companion opportunity to tell himself why. Younger children and older adults outside the perimeters of the formal learning setting have been excluded from an educational process which has become mandated as the rite of passage, and repassage, through the heart of the community.

Society's increasingly jaundiced view of education is not without foundation in fact, for it has witnessed countless innovations in curriculum and methodology, listened patiently to goal redefinition, and even entered into a tentative dialogue — at the risk of repeating a short-term relationship that is fraught with condescension on the part of school personnel. In spite of this historical pattern, the institutions of family, business, industry, labor, and government continually reaffirm their faith in education's potential. They are less awed now and expect more from their schools, simply because they have equaled, and in some cases surpassed, the educator's ability to assess the reality each adolescent must eventually face.

That reality is neither cold nor inflexible, but is one for which few of our present high school or college graduates are prepared. The collective focus upon education's abstract richness, at the expense of its definition as a tool, has created a needless schism between the school and society. By defining "preparation for work" as a time- and setting-based activity, limited to a secondary school's vocational course offerings, education has contradicted its own developmental premise. This contradiction has resulted in the individual's loss of control over the options available but unknown to him, and has too often left him ill-prepared for his potential role in a progress- and profit-oriented economy.

These conditions are not restricted to the young, the poor, and the black, but have become a general malady. With the discovery that too many of our young people are later found engaging in life and work as if they were alien cultures, education is being challenged by society to assure not only the acquisition of basic academic skills, but the vocational preparedness and social adjustment of its children as well.

If the nature of work is to become more harmonious with the goals of the individual, every individual must have more knowledge of himself and the world of work. All work does not have dignity . . . nor does it always reward and uplift the person who does it. Only people can define or change the quality of work they do. The elementary schools have an unparalleled opportunity to confront this fact of life in such a way that young people develop a well-based optimism about their eventual capacity for influencing the character of the work they choose. That optimism is not based only on the child's short memory of achievement; it is developed and maintained by his unobstructed view of numerous desirable alternatives. Because their alternatives derive from identification with real people, children require a constant and tactile association with divergent life-styles in order to begin the process of determining their own. Candid admission that school personnel alone cannot provide all the human and experiential resources each child needs in order to seek, find, and experience a satisfying working role can and will motivate society to share those resources.

It is true that an initially positive intimacy has always existed between a community and its elementary schools. But as children grow older, and educational content becomes more abstract, that intimacy disappears. It is as if educators say to the parent and to the businessman: "We have noted your presence, now pay us and leave us alone to get down to the business of education!" This loss of intimacy is not only our children's loss, but has profound implications for the working community surrounding them. Silencing expertise is as effective as denouncing it, and no working man of woman fails to get this message from those schools which exclude them from the educational process. The stronger of these individuals will counter with stoicism, criticism, or even contempt, but the great majority will accept education's definition of their passive role, and will, through their fulfillment of it, perpetuate the school-community gap career education hopes to eradicate.

For well over a decade, concerned professionals in the fields of counseling, manpower, and economics — as well as in education — have pursued a refocusing of education. They speak of a restructuring which would alleviate the malaise of those who find work to be at odds with their uninformed perceptions of it. An impediment to educational reform even more obstructive than the tie of teachers and educators to their past experiences is the tendency to argue education objectives as moral, even theological issues rather than pragmatic ones. To discover that society is *not* threatened by the concepts of career education, but is in fact urging these changes adds credence to its potential as a force which could re-engage and involve the entire community.

Assigning to the schools the coordinating role in career education's implementation can broaden and deepen the educational process in a liaison of which the child will not be the sole beneficiary. The working adult could also receive, as well as contribute to educational experiences which specify no age criterion for their access. In an exercise which spans a lifetime — that of exploring, choosing, preparing for, and engaging in one or more career alternatives — children will and must question the purpose of education and work, and believable adults must respond to those questions. The task of locating such expertise will require a concerted effort on the parts of school personnel, not because believable adults are in short supply, but because educators have rarely found occasion to recognize the community as more than a complex of services responding to their needs. To overcome decades of the kind of institutionalized behavior which has had schools alternately commanding or ignoring the attention of their communities, educators will have to make a well-publicized, albeit humble, exit from their sanctuaries in this search for strong colleagues.

Because authenticity and skill are seldom announced on office doors, store fronts, factory gates, or on peoples' work clothes, school personnel will find it both necessary and rewarding to listen to, observe, and question people who work in every conceivable setting. While this process should be a continuing one, the immediate task of convening a group of on-the-line career experts is best served through the nominations by their spokesmen, through such agencies as chambers of commerce, government offices, union and apprenticeship councils, churches and hospitals, parent and service clubs, private foundations, and retired citizen groups. The good, open publicity attendant upon this search can bring together the resources of the media, and will often resolve in the creation or assignment of a community-based ombudsman who can continue to articulate both the needs and the skills of that community as they relate to the educative process.

Once established, a bona fide community effort is dependent upon unwavering focus on the goal for which it exists. Educators will have to entertain the possibility that academic endurance on their parts will be a less important team credential than will the human and avocational skills they can combine with the variety of life-styles and work environments provided by their colleagues. By the same token, the most credible advocacy for the acquisition of the basic academic skills they must impart will come, not from themselves, but from those same colleagues.

An advantage of career education's team approach is that it forces each member — whether teacher, carpenter, or paramedic — to step outside his own static estate and begin to learn again. No klieg light is as bright and direct as the child who comes unerringly to the point: "Why did you pick the job you have? If it's a good job, why do you look so sad? If it's a bad job, why don't you change it . . . or leave it? What does it take for me to grow up to be someone just like you?" Few adults have asked these questions of themselves or each other, and many would find it necessary to do some soul searching before the answers could come. There is no initial team bond as strong as that discovery of a common history in the majority of working adults . . . a history marked by a Topsy-like pattern of stumbling toward a career goal and being lucky, or unlucky enough to achieve it.

Career education's premise — that children must know their options and have the time and opportunity to choose wisely among them — has resulted in a near universal agreement that the reality-accident route to work must revert to a historical archetype . . . remembered but not repeated.

Suggestions for Further Reading

Banta, Trudy W.; and Marshall, Patricia. "Bringing Schools and In-
    dustry Together." *Manpower* 2 (June 1970):24–41.
Boocock, Sarane; and Schild, E. O., Editors. *Simulation Games in
    Learning*. Beverly Hills, California: Sage, 1968.
Bruner, Jerome. "The Process of Education Revisited." *Phi Delta
    Kappan* (September 1971).
Hamilton, Jack A.; and Krumboltz, John D. "Simulated Work Experi-
    ence: How Realistic Should It Be?" *Personnel and Guidance Jour-
    nal* 48:1 (September 1969).

5

Home and Family in Career Education

In chapter 1 we showed how education and work as basic values in American society are in peril. The family is much more basic and more troubled in its role and values. Increasingly it is recognized that many, if not most of the social and personal issues with which educators wrestle daily are problems emerging within the home and emanating from the failure of the family experience to inculcate the values and develop the skills necessary to function successfully in the society. The whole of the educational effort seems unable to generally overcome and dispel the handicaps of inadequate early environment. Yet that recognition does not and cannot justify retreat.

Homes which have serious weaknesses are least capable of reforming themselves. The family has its own educational needs, and education, particularly elementary education, cannot fill its role without the support of home and family. This is as true of career education as it is of any other aspect of education's many objectives. This chapter explores the desirable role of home and family in career development for young children. However, since this book is addressed primarily to the elementary school teacher, its first intent is to suggest ways that the elementary school can supplement and strengthen the role of home and family.

Rationale for the Home and Family Component

Traditionally, the family has been a closely knit, compact unit, the cornerstone for building a composite society. It has been there that human interactions were first observed and experienced and values developed. There work as a concept and a fact of life was also observed, participated in, and attitudes toward it and skills for it developed. However, the structure of our society and the nature of our living patterns make it less likely that children today will acquire major segments of their value systems from the family unit. This factor is particularly true for work values, but in some cases, may be too true for education values. Children seldom have the opportunity to see their parents in work settings, to say nothing of working alongside their parents, as was the case when much of the economy had an agricultural base. And although parents may discuss their work in the home, they seldom talk about the positive aspects of it, verbalizing instead their complaints and disappointments. Children seldom perceive the creative expression their parents derive from work since they cannot glimpse the total picture of what the work setting offers in terms of personal development and satisfaction. The abstract, work-associated values of loyalty, punctuality, job advancement, or performance compensation are vague and difficult for children to understand. Thus they fail to develop the idea that work can be a privilege and an opportunity.

A similar problem exists with education, for as educational facilities and personnel become more remote from the home, parents tend to become less involved in day-to-day processes of education. School, work, and home life have become three separate activities which are never integrated into one systematic, value-producing unit as once they were. As a result of these and other factors, many families rear children who do not value work as a generator of satisfaction and pride of achievement. Other families do not perceive education as possible for them and related to their economic welfare.

In the interets of the individual and his society, it becomes important that education does not usurp the role of the family in creating values. Instead, education should seek to complement this role, not only by providing guidance but also by involving the entire family in the educational process. If education attempts to replace the family as the unit for teaching values, it will contribute to the breakdown of the family unit while increasing the problems inherent in value formation. On the other hand, where the family lacks the strength to fill its role, education is one of the social institutions most available to buttress it or to substitute for more of its functions.

The demands for more parent involvement in school are increasing. Parent groups are becoming alarmed by rising costs in education, many federal programs are requiring parent participation, and research findings continue to demonstrate the importance of the early years of childhood in cognitive and affective development. Research continues to point out the importance of the parent as the first educator of the child, as well as the effect of the home as the first classroom of the child.

Our purpose here is to explore ways in which the elementary school might support the home and family in making more positive and meaningful their contributions to the career development process. Together with that exploration, we shall discuss techniques through which the home and family can add dimension to the education process by cooperating with and supporting the school in the area of career education. All of this may require some changes in the attitudes of parents toward the school; it will require basic shifts in the teachers' approach to the needs of the students, particularly at the elementary school level.

If the elementary school teacher is to understand the children he teaches, he must see them as part of family units. Within the family, the child, mother, and father have all embarked on careers — all have different roles to perform. The child is in the school phase of his career. The mother's career may be twofold, encompassing a working role outside the home with the role of homemaker within the home. Likewise the father may have a twofold role, working both outside and within the home to support the family as he plays a father and homemaking role. If the teacher ignores the family unit and attempts to see and work with the child as an isolated case, hostility might be created within those parents being excluded from the educational process.

With cooperation of parents and educators, a child's chance to learn can be greatly enhanced. Educators must take the lead to establish relationships by inviting parents to school and by home visits to exchange ideas. Progress may be slow at first, but continued attempts of working with parents by involving them in such ways as resource persons, volunteer helpers to create materials, or organizers of activities will bring results as parents will gain an understanding of what the school is doing, while educators receive an understanding of how the school can assist the home as a learning center.

As an example of the kinds of changes that will be necessary, we can point to the field of home economics. The need for change is evidenced by society's reluctant but increasing acknowledgment that women should be afforded the same opportunities for career satisfaction as men have always enjoyed, whether that career be in the home or outside it or, as is increasingly likely, in a combination of homemaking and professional pursuits. In response to this change in the attitudes of society, home economics education has taken on the new terminology of "family living" with the resultant move away from its concentration on teaching cooking and sewing into other vital homemaking skills such as budgeting, efficient use of time, child care, relating to people, and other subjects. Family living no longer can be concerned with only maintenance-type tasks in the home, but in its expanded role must cover all aspects of life in the home, as well as life outside the home. In addition, more emphasis must be placed on attracting male students to home economics classes as the male assumes more and more of the homemaking responsibilities in his role as father and family member.

Another area of drastic change which has received all too little attention is the economic role of the family. Once regarded as a productive unit of society, the family has become primarily a consuming unit, a buyer of goods and services produced by professional individuals or large industrial organizations. And yet there is virtually no educational training to prepare individuals for the consumer role. As a result, members of our society often consume irrationally or make poor decisions in the selection of goods. Family life education can logically be expanded to include a large component of consumer education in order to better prepare all members of the family for this role.

This one small example is just an indication of what can and must be done if education is to assume its responsibilities in our society. Consumer education should not be a subject limited only to home economics . . . it should also be a concern of such courses as mathematics, sociology, psychology, history, economics, and even English, where the literature of consumer consciousness might be equally as valuable a teaching tool as traditional storybooks.

As the purpose of career education is to prepare people to become meaningful members of society, students and their parents should receive training in decision making. Educators can assist parents in this area by helping them to understand that children must gain experience in making their own decisions. They also need the opportunity of learning the consequences of their decisions and should be allowed to make mistakes so that they can benefit from their errors. As decision making is a process, students need activities both in the school and in the home which will provide them with the opportunity of considering alternatives, gathering and organizing information, and making choices. Through cooperation of teachers and parents, children can learn the process of decision making which will lay the groundwork for career choices.

Career education — whether concerned with the career of a homemaker, a laborer, or a professional person — has as one of its fundamental principles the concept that all classes at all levels of society have a career component. In this chapter, we are concerned with the essential reinforcing partnership between the home and the school, and the mutual roles they each have in teaching home and family living, consumer education, and work values. Since more teachers than parents are likely to read this book, we emphasize those things that the elementary school teacher can do to reinforce the child's positive attitude toward the home and family as an integral part of career education.

Building the Foundation

It is in the home that the child first observes the basic characteristics that signify the final denouement of his or her life: the role of work as an essential element for sustaining life and the inevitability that the rewards of work produce the necessities of life and let us maintain comfortable surroundings. The role of mutual cooperation and service and the sharing of responsibility are observed and absorbed from infancy. The attitudes of parents and siblings toward work responsibilities within the home are rapidly internalized by the young child. The role of outsiders in contributing to the commodities and services of the home and the necessity, in most cases, of one or both parents working outside the home to earn money to pay for those commodities and services are subsequent realizations. That satisfaction and pride of achievement can emerge from work within and outside of the home will be realized and absorbed by the child only if they are demonstrated by the parents.

The home is a workshop, a learning laboratory, a consuming unit, and an inculcator of values. The family's function is to provide a setting within which the individual can develop a sense of security, of belonging, and of acceptance as a person; it is a place for relaxation, for expression, and for control of emotion; it teaches the child to experience success and to absorb failure; and it helps the child develop a value system by observing and sharing experiences with others. These early experiences can be positive or negative; but whichever they are, they will influence the child for life in the world of work — as well as in other endeavors.

Teaching Home and Family Living

If work can be defined as "productive contribution," whether or not it is compensated within the labor market, home and family living has career aspects, not only for homemakers, but for both parents and all other family members. Society can gain by broadening the opportunities for women to fulfill themselves and contribute to a society through every possible career of interest to them. But society can also gain by adding to the prestige and satisfactions of homemaking as a woman's career, whether as a primary activity or in tandem with a job outside the home. Similarly, society suffers as parental responsibility and homemaking are ignored or neglected as career concerns of men. If, as has been said of external careers for men and women who have assumed such responsibilities, "no success can compensate for failure within the home," why is there so little attention to preparation for home responsibility?

"Home economics" is still the largest single component of vocational education. Yet it continues to suffer criticism and to slip in prestige, primarily because it has been limited to cooking and sewing — hardly the most vital of homemaking skills — and has been limited to female students. For many years, home economists have attempted to shore up this slipping prestige by stressing preparation for occupations by teaching in conjunction with home economics such related skills as food service and child care. Only recently has this educational component broadened its curriculum to include consumer education (primarily for female heads of households), with emphasis on those in poverty situations.

Successful home and family living involves skills far beyond those of cooking and sewing. The latter has become largely recreational in modern society, and the former is constantly being simplified. As women demand greater recognition and opportunity to exercise their individual creativity and their minds, talents, and skills, they rightly ask: Why are the monotonous, repetitious rudiments of housekeeping exclusively female tasks? Only the biological functions of gestation, birth, and nursing the baby are the obvious sex-limited roles for women. Men daily fulfill their stereotyped, male-oriented roles as breadwinners, often stifling a propensity for combining homemaking skills with their outside careers.

Parenthood is work, and it requires profound attention to detail if it is to be successful. It is a male as well as a female career; yet both sexes combine parenthood with other career roles. As with other careers, parental responsibility must be learned; but it can be taught, both within and outside the home or the school. The years of elementary schooling, a stage at which the child is more closely associated with parents than in subsequent years, is none too soon for children to become aware of their potential roles as parents and the skills which these roles will entail. Observing parents in action will be the primary means of absorbing insights about these roles; but classroom discussion and application can advance understanding from the intuitive to the explicit. The child can come to articulate the type of parent he would like to be and begin to transform those attributes into characteristics. One suggested activity toward the end of this chapter will aid the child (with the help of the parents and teachers) to become aware of and start to conceive of himself in the parent role.

Consumer Education

If we are to prepare our children to function adequately in the world of work, as well as within the family framework, we must be sure that career education focuses on the family as a basic unit for consuming goods and services. The success of the family in balancing its income for purchasing its necessary goods and budgeting for recreational and other purposes has a great effect upon the stability and happiness of the family members. The elementary school teacher can assist the child and family in this matter by providing a program in consumer education.

During the elementary school years, children form their basic attitudes about earning and spending money. Teachers can provide classroom experiences for children by setting up situations that will give students a chance to become involved in money management. For example, they can design experiences in mathematics classes wherein students can learn about common family expenditures and budgeting. Wherever possible, the educator should attempt to relate the learning of the student in school with his life outside of school. The educator can assign the student to complete a project by shopping for groceries with his parents. The student could be provided with a budget and could find out what he must do to stay within it while meeting family needs. Likewise students could gain valuable experience by participating with parents in buying appliances, furniture, cars, or other major purchases. As well as learning to make decisions in purchasing, the student could gain knowledge about methods of payment, maintenance features, guarantees, etc.

To help children gain knowledge and experience of how family income is obtained, the teacher can provide a "business" lesson for the class. Indeed, the lesson could be far-reaching if several teachers combined their classes to set up a "mock" bank, a grocery store, or a shopping center (with methods adapted to local situations). By following through in this cooperative venture, students would have first-hand knowledge in profit and loss, wages, budgeting, and other fundamentals of business.

To tie the consumer education prográm to the home situations of the students, the teacher(s) could use parents as resource personnel to give greater personal meaning to the business experience. The parents could suggest situations for the students to "act out" the work roles of actual workaday world people, drawing on their own experiences in their jobs as material for the "play." The same visits by the students to employing establishments in the community to observe the nature of the world of work could be used to emphasize work as the source of family income. In addition, the elementary school teacher can prepare students as consumers by providing role-playing situations in the classroom where boys and girls plan a family's or an individual's budget or allowance.

Development of Work Values

During early childhood, an individual's self-concept is molded, and the workaday world plays a significant part in its formation. The home serves as a world of work laboratory for vocational development wherein children's attitudes, values, and goals are initially formed. By observing such home service personnel as milk and mail deliverers, television repair technicians, plumbers, and the like, children soon pattern their "play" experiences after these observations. From the world of work outside the home, they develop concepts of the nurse, the doctor, the law enforcement officer, the grocery clerk, and so forth.

Children listen to their parents and siblings express points of view about people in various occupations, thus acquiring their families' attitudes toward occupations. They soon learn to think of some occupations as valuable and some as valueless. Their inherent opinions of these occupations cling to them as they mature. Parents have a great deal to do with determining children's basic attitudes toward work . . . whether they will be work oriented or indolent, whether they will seek responsibility or avoid it, whether they will look upon work as an opportunity for growth or as drudgery. By observing their parents, children learn attitudes about gaining education or training, earning and spending money, enjoying esthetic experiences, doing different types of work, incorporating religious beliefs into their lives, and relating to others. The parents serve as models for children, with the youngsters absorbing values and goals their parents deem most important. A child may later accept or reject parents' attitudes and values, but the parents' orientation will have a great influence on the child's life.

Siblings also affect the child's vocational development. If an older brother or sister has done particularly well or has dismally failed in school or in a career, the influence on the younger child is manifested in the child's behavior toward the world of work. If there is strong rivalry between or among siblings, the child may avoid doing those things the brother or sister did. Conversely, if there are strong ties, the child may pattern his or her life after the older sibling.

Parents' occupations significantly influence the ways in which their children develop. If the father is a businessman, he will react to any family situation in a business-oriented manner; e.g., if he is primarily concerned with profit and loss, there will be a carryover of this concept into the home where it might affect the family budget, recreational activities, intrapersonal relationships, and even religious orientation. In short, the child will see the father dress as a businessman, speak as a businessman, act as a businessman, and in truth *be* a businessman. And the child's life will be in some manner oriented toward the world of business.

Similarly, if the child's mother is a schoolteacher, her occupation will influence the way that she relates to her own children. Because her training and work are oriented toward educational principles, she will incorporate the knowledge, attitudes, and experiences gained through her profession into her role as a mother. Thus the child's development will have been influenced by the parent's threefold role as homemaker, parent, and teacher.

Few would doubt that parents exercise the greatest single influence upon educational and career choices of their children. Yet, though most parents are aware of their responsibilities to their children, they have little concept of how they can aid in their children's career development. Parents express frustration at not knowing how to instill within their children the desire to want to work or to want to learn how to work. They often indicate that they do not know how to talk to their children in regard to future career roles. The schoolteacher may be able to help parents with these problems. The family and school can work together to convey work values to the youngster.

Elementary school children are in the "fantasy" stage of career exploration, where they see themselves performing tasks of various workers without identifying abilities or interests related to occupations. In this beginning stage of discovery, learning can be greatly enhanced if parents will create within the home an atmosphere that will enable a child to experiment with many occupations. Through work in the home, the child can be exposed to many careers if parents are alert to the relationship of the tasks in the home to the world of work. (For example, a child could learn about the field of interior decorating by becoming involved in buying or repairing furniture and making room arrangements in the home. An informed parent could assist the child to learn about this field by explaining decorating principles and by involving him in decisions and work that must be performed.) There are a multitude of tasks in the home relating to the working world which can assist the child to learn about such jobs as carpentry, taking care of a yard, purchasing, interior designing, chauffering, budgeting, restaurant and hotel work, education, health or medicine, mechanics, and so forth.

Not only can a child learn about types of work, he can also learn basic attitudes and values associated with work. Since the child will develop attitudes and values whether or not a deliberate attempt is made to teach them, the result may not be positive. The home can provide the setting wherein the child can learn to follow directions, work under authority, develop responsibility for accomplishing tasks, develop initiative to work without being told to do so, and complete each task he begins. However, the home can instill opposing values in the child if the parents continually express negative attitudes about work. "What a week! I'm glad it's Friday." "Back to the old salt mine." "You didn't do as you were told. Now you must scrub the floor as punishment!" None of these comments do much to make work seem worthwhile.

Parental involvement is particularly important in career exploration because the nature of today's society has removed many opportunities for parents and youth to work together. The era of the family farm or business has essentially expired. Few of today's youth know what kinds of jobs their parents hold or what they do when they get to their place of work. S. I. Hayakawa, President of San Francisco State College, said:

> To become a man, it has always been necessary for boys to associate with men, as helpers on father's farm, as apprentices to craftsmen, as squires to knights, as water-boys to baseball teams. Through such associations, they learn the secrets of the adult culture; what rituals to observe, how to care for equipment . . . how to earn and maintain the respect of other men in a society of men. But today most boys are separated from the lives of men. Men leave for factory or office in the morning, commuting many miles to work. They do not return until evening. Boys are brought up by mothers and schoolteachers. Hence, boys often have no idea what their fathers do at work. They have no idea what a man does that makes him a man.[1]

Yet self-evident as this statement is, it contains its own anachronisms which must be dispelled. Girls see mother primarily in her homemaking role, and rarely see other women in occupations other than teachers, nurses, or clerical workers. Opportunities must be established for them to perceive possibilities beyond the traditional stereotypes.

Just as the family business or farm is on its way to obscurity, so also is the era of the family as a self-sustaining unit. When once a family raised its own foods, made its own clothing, provided its own shelter, it has now entered an age of specialization in services and products. Rarely are parents involved in making or growing anything for the fam-

---

[1] S. I. Hayakawa, "On the Other Hand," *Saturday Evening Post*, Spring 1972.

ily. Instead, they are able to buy products and services without their children having a knowledge of how these products are manufactured or how service skills are learned. Lacking perspective on many types of work, parents are unable to teach their youngsters about work that involves family needs. Their own work has become so specialized that it is often only one segment in the manufacture, distribution, and dissemination of a product or service. Thus the educator can perform a vital service for the family by assisting children to understand how to relate modern-day services to various types of careers.

There is no fundamental principle of work itself that cannot be easily demonstrated in the home. It is in the home where children are first introduced to such concepts as the interdependence of workers on each other for successful production, the importance of cooperation among those who work together, the nature of specialization of work roles, the need for punctuality if a task is to be completed on time, the desirability of cleanliness in the work area, the necessity for accepting personal responsibility for performance of assigned tasks, the urgency of following instructions, and the value of avoiding unnecessary waste. Other concepts can be learned also . . . the boredom one feels in performing a routine task, even though it might be an important link in a chain of assembly-line tasks, or the reprimands that are typically a part of the world of work if a worker fails to perform his assigned task correctly. Yet these negative results can be mitigated by a self-awareness that the rewards which come from successful completion of an assigned task are worth the extra time and effort.

While these values *can* be learned in the home, and while some work values will inevitably be learned there and elsewhere, it is difficult for parents to expose their children to a representative vista of the world of work. First, children and parents no longer find many occasions to work side by side in normal work settings. Second, it is no longer likely that the family will purchase such items as furniture that was made in the "shop down the street" where children can see the craftsman at work. Instead, the family purchases furniture — and most other items — without having any knowledge of how it was constructed and often with little knowledge of (and little concern about) what types of material have gone into the construction. For these reasons, it is important that teachers become involved in the vital role of assisting children to learn about their parents' work, both to understand more about work and more about their parents.

ATTITUDES OF PARENTS

For career education objectives to be realized, it is essential that parents become aware of how attitudes in the home affect their children's orientation to the working world. Efforts should be made to adopt, change, or modify parental attitudes relating to career education. As a first step, the teacher must become aware of the home-influenced attitudes — be they purposefully instilled or only vicariously obtained — which are related to work. If possible, such attitudes should be accepted because they may be practicable and workable for the family. Also if possible, the career education program should be modified to include these attitudes, thus resulting in a working relationship between the home and the school.

Youth are unlikely to have a positive attitude about work unless their parents do. Unfortunately, many people still look upon work as did the ancient civilizations, viewing it as curse or drudgery and placing little value on promoting it to improve the national character. The Bible laments the driving of Adam and Eve from the Garden of Eden, whereupon man had to earn his bread by the sweat of his brow. In early Greek, Roman, and other cultures, work was done by the lower classes or by slaves; an individual was born into his occupational class, where the higher classes received no training in common tasks; rulers were given the craft at the top of the hierarchical ordering, with workers at the bottom. Freedom of choice was nonexistent.

Today work need no longer be a drudgery to the majority of working people. Ideally, the individual has an opportunity to understand his own capabilities and likes and to select a career related to these. Few must work only to exist. It is through work that an individual achieves maturity and experiences satisfaction, accomplishment, and joy in earning an income — and learns to express himself.

It is the responsibility of the family to impress upon the child the idea that work is a privilege and not a drudgery. The teaching of this attitude can be one of the most important tasks of the family. Cartoonist Charles Schulz may have Snoopy complain, "Work is the crabgrass in the lawn of life," but work — for pay, for service to self and to others, or for avocation, coupled with leisure — comprises that lawn. Elementary school teachers can assist parents in acquiring the attitude that work is good, as well as essential in a youngster's life.

Though some successful parents, having experienced hardships in their upward struggle to their present position in life, wish to spare their children these experiences, they fail to realize that these struggles may be the very lessons that developed their ability to achieve. Far too many parents believe that if they could make life easier for their children than it was for them, the children would somehow be better off . . . as if the ideal would be to create a condition under which the children would never have to work. This attitude is diametrically opposed to what we know and can predict about work in our society. The preservation of some form of work ethic and work values serves as an underlying goal of career education because it is necessary to the successful interrelationships of that society. Parents who take pride in their children's aspirations for work and successful performance of work tasks, no matter how small, are teaching concepts that are essential to our future.

This concept was illustrated by Socrates who interviewed a prospective student by asking: "Can you cook your own meals?"

"No," the student said, "we have servants for doing that."

"Well," Socrates continued, "can you make your own sandals?"

"No," the student replied, "we have servants for doing that."

Socrates then asked, "Can you make your own toga?"

"No," the student said, "we have servants for doing that also."

"Isn't it a shame," Socrates replied, "that we teach our servants better than we teach our own children."

It is vital that youngsters become involved in work, and parents can create work projects which will give children needed work experiences. All too often parents shake their heads in despair when children fail to complete assigned work tasks. Teachers can counsel parents in involving children in tasks around the home, explaining the following principles, which are common counsel in employer-employee relationships, but are usually neglected with children:

(1) Parents should realize that children gain most from a work project when they understand the entire scope of a task. Children are often given only menial tasks without fully comprehending the entirety of the job; therefore, they regard their jobs

as dull, gain the idea that work is a punishment or a drudge, and avoid it wherever possible. If the child is able to see the gestalt, the wholeness of a task, from the reasoning, planning, execution, and evaluation stages, he is more likely to understand and appreciate the scope of the project. For example, children often dread the task of emptying the trash. However, if they receive an orientation of the relationship of this task to health or medicine and are provided with an opportunity to role-play tasks of those in medical professions, the job can be regarded as important and fun for the child. At the same time, the child has increased his knowledge about careers.

(2) Parents should involve their children in creative work projects. Though they are often concerned that their children seem to regard work as a drudgery, parents sometimes fail to create work projects that would interest their children and provide them with valuable work experience. The following examples could be cited by the elementary school teacher in a parent-teacher conference to induce parents to create work projects in their own families:

(a) One family, desiring a work project to foster family togetherness, organized a "Shower Club," electing officers and holding business meetings. The purpose of the work project was to install a shower in their home. Involving all the family, the club members planned how to raise funds and how to arrange for the shower's construction. Each member gained knowledge of work as a carpenter by watching the father cut, saw, and nail the pieces of lumber. They learned what a plumber has to do to connect new pipes to old inlets and outlets, and they became adept as painters when the father and mother allowed them to handle the paintbrushes — with much coaching from the parents. In addition, they obtained some slight knowledge of accounting as they totaled their budget and subtracted payments for the lumber, paint, plumbing fixtures, and so forth. When the project was finished, the parents were gratified to find that their children were imbued with a new attitude . . . that work is challenging, even exciting, and well worth the effort.

(b) In another family where the father is a physician, the parents were concerned that their children were leading a too-easy existence. The parents wished to instill a respect for manual labor in their offspring lest they grew up thinking that "work" meant only a profession and the duties imposed by a profession. They assigned manual tasks for which the children were responsible, in the home and at the office, and were keen to make certain that these tasks were carried out to the smallest detail. Because they wanted the children to learn the value of money as well as the value of manual work, they paid in definite amounts for the work done. The children not only received valuable hands-on experiences from these tasks, they earned a regular income with an added knowledge of the worth of their contributions.

(3) Children will have a stronger positive outlook on work and will put a greater effort into their tasks when they are provided with "time off." Even as adults enjoy vacations, children also look forward to them. If they are given a day off each week, free from housework, they will be more likely to enjoy work the remainder of the week, and following their day off, will accomplish their assigned work with increased desire and motivation.

(4) To use work as a punishment can only diminish the attractiveness of work as a concept. The same is true of insistence on work for work's sake, simply because the parent feels that the child ought to work. Some tasks may be intrinsically enjoyable; but for most tasks, the satisfaction comes from some form of achievement through work. It is that achievement which will be stressed by the wise parents.

Through a career education program, teachers can assist parents in recognizing as a fallacy the myth that all children must pursue a college education in order to be successful. The schools will not be successful in conveying the message that occupations and educational alternatives differ only in the kind and not in the innate work if parents are convinced of the contrary. Far too many parents seem ashamed of the work that they do and of the type of preparation it required. Unless their own self-esteem is restored, they will pass on similar negative attitudes to their children. Such attitudes can only harm the next generation's self-esteem, especially if parental expectations are not fulfilled. Equally dangerous is the attitude of "looking down upon" those less prestigious occupations. If children do not undertake those occupations themselves, they must live with and should respect those who do.

Through consultations, the elementary school teacher can determine if parents have unrealistic or unreasonable expectations for their children. Then instead of scolding the parents for their expectations, the teacher may help the parents reorient their thinking by involving the child and parents in activities related to the child's interests and abilities. A self-explanatory activity which could assist the parents in learning the likes, dislikes, abilities, and interests of the child could then be implemented in the home.

PARENTAL INVOLVEMENT

Because the involvement of parents with the school is of paramount importance to career education programs, the elementary school teacher must actively seek parental participation. In formulating such a program, the teacher may wish to consider the following suggestions:

(1) The teacher should gain a knowledge of the students' backgrounds and home situations, learning of parents' occupations and their orientation toward the world of work. This can be accomplished in the following manner:

(a) Each child can be encouraged to find out what his parents do in the working world, and through role-playing and show-and-tell procedures, can share his feelings and ideas with classmates.

(b) Parent-teacher conferences and associations which provide opportunities for teachers to consult with parents are the most obvious, direct route to reach the parents. During these consultations, the teacher who is sensitive to the vagaries of parental attitudes can deduce from the feedback how the parents would respond to the career education program.

(2) If it is difficult to involve parents in the above activities, the teacher can often reach them by generating enthusiasm in the children. If the teacher can plan an activity that involves all students in the classroom, and if he can provide the opportunity for the parents to see their children as active participants, most parents will find themselves willing to become involved.

(3) Teachers may wish to communicate with parents through newsletters or circulars. Positive classroom work experiences that have happened to the children can be related via the newsletter to the parents to give additional impetus to the parents' involvement.

(4) Many parents instinctively become irrepressibly enthusiastic about their children's school experiences. The teacher should search out these parents as public relations-type personnel for spreading the word and recruiting other parents into the program.

(5) Because mothers usually spend more time with their children than fathers, personal contact between the teacher and mother is vital. Inviting groups of mothers to visit the school could enable the teacher to explain the advantages of relating activities at home to career exploration and could also pinpoint for the mothers those areas in which their children have special interests or sensitivities. Through these personal contacts, the family could help the child develop positive work attitudes.

(6) In special instances where permission has been granted by managers, supervisors, owners, and the like, teachers could — if they feel that such drastic measures are necessary in the interests of the child — visit parents at work locations to discuss the child's education progress while becoming acquainted with the work of the parents.

Because many parents are not aware of how they can use the home to expose youngsters to work, teachers can encourage involvement and offer guidance to help families set up small business enterprises to increase the child's hands-on knowledge of the business world. For instance, if an elementary school-age boy or girl wishes to sample the real world of work, he or she could establish a "small business" with a door-to-door distribution of goods, such as delivering newspapers or magazines or selling bakery goods, or with a service, such as cutting lawns, running errands for a small fee, or baby-sitting for short periods of time during the day. To make the enterprise more meaningful to the child, the entire family can be involved in the experience:

(1) An older child or the parents could help in the actual delivery of the newspapers or magazines, or could accompany the young student when errands mean a trip to the grocery store or drugstore. The added dimension of helping him find the correct address for the magazines or newspapers or the special brand specified by the "client" at the drugstore could be rewarding to parents and child.

(2) The father or mother could reinforce the child's knowledge of mathematics by helping with the "profit and loss" aspect of the venture, the joy of any bonus work, and the counting of the proceeds after "collection time" each week or month. Setting aside money as a savings account or letting it accrue for any worthwhile spending — the well-known "rainy day" — is an experience that would instill a commendable attribute in any child.

(3) Any family member can help "expand" the business by recruiting new customers, but because very young children are often plagued with excessive timidity (though some display temerity), an older child or one of the parents should accompany the child at first.

(4) The importance of giving good quality work, of "going the extra mile" for a customer, can instill in the child the resulting joy that can be felt from "doing the job right."

(5) The family work project can be an ongoing accomplishment, offering any child new responsibilities as he matures and is able to perform new and more difficult tasks.

Parents and Teachers as Partners

Many parents are not aware of how they can use the home setting to reinforce their child's learning in school. If the elementary school teacher can involve the parents in career education activities, the combination of home and school working together for a common purpose accomplishes a great deal more than either factor working separately. As a part of the regular responsibilities of a teacher, time should be scheduled for parent-teacher programs. To facilitate this, it must be viewed by the school administration as a legitimate function of the teacher's responsibility, with released time being provided to carry it out. This is a very legitimate program since a child's learning will be enhanced by involving him in not only classroom experiences but applications in the home as well. Generally speaking, teachers have not been trained to work with parents, at least not to any extensive degree. Therefore, techniques of involving and motivating parents should be a component of programs to train teachers in career education.

As teachers meet with parents, one of the primary goals should be to have parents understand that they should provide decision-making experiences for their children. A model of the decision-making process can occur in the parent-teacher meetings by planning to have parents actively participate in projects and activities. It will also be well to have students participate in strategic sessions of meetings so that a combination of the educative team — parents, children, and teachers — can be involved in working together. This may be developed further by using older children as members of the team to work with younger children. To make the experience realistic, teachers should provide children with the opportunity of working alone and with others, for this is the situation that will most likely occur in life.

At first, the teachers may be reluctant to ask the parents to become involved in affairs of the classroom. Some teachers feel that the school should not interfere in the home, and vice versa. However, if teachers can join with parents as partners in career education activities, the opportunities for the child's potential development will be greatly enhanced. A recent study in parent-teacher cooperation reveals that:

> A teacher working in an area where parents almost always cooperate, as compared with a teacher working in an area of little or no parent cooperation, is six times as likely to say that his pupils are exceptionally well-behaved. . . . It appears from the data collected that close parent-teacher teamwork offers one of the best solutions to school behavior problems ever devised.[2]

---

[2] Carol and Harry Smallenburg, "School Behavior — Whose Problem?" *PTA Magazine* (February 1971).

Involvement of parents in the classroom career education program will not happen overnight. When parents have been called in for conferences by teachers, it has usually been for evaluative or disciplinary reasons which have resulted in a threatening experience for parents. This troubled atmosphere will need to be changed to one of a cooperative nature before the conference can be successful. Any suspicions held by either side must be alleviated . . . a difficult task that will require initiative from the elementary school teacher. Though parents may be defensive at first, they will respond if they are treated as equal partners — and they can become a powerful force for strengthening career education objectives.

Once convinced of the merits of career education, parents can become a valuable ally to the teacher. Today's parents are better prepared than ever before to help make a major change in the American education system. Many of them will have special interests in career education, for they have been involved in the pressures and forces that have effected the need for it. In addition, they are better educated, better informed, and better prepared to participate in the education of their children. (The average parent today has one year of education beyond high school.) Parents of the near future will likely have increased education, with involvement in courses in family living, psychology, and sociology. Such preparation will assist these parents in becoming intellectual equals with the teacher or counselor and more capable partners in career education.

Programs must be tailored to fit the local situation, taking into consideration the strengths of the teacher, the income of the family, the employment of the parents, the interests and needs of the children, and the composition, religious orientation, social status, and geographical location of the families. Commuter teachers, larger numbers of married women with family responsibilities as elementary school teachers, complicated family situations, and other factors will require individual programs. However, within the flexibility of career education, there is a program which can be developed for every situation.

Because the early childhood home environment has a profound effect on every aspect of later life, it is important that education strengthen home and family living by what is taught in the school. It is vital for children to explore basic concepts of learning how to interact with others

in the elementary grades. Building on this foundation in the secondary
school years, the students can then focus on learning to develop a family
structure that is stable and will withstand the pressures of the modern
world.

Because the composition of families will vary greatly according to
local conditions and customs, the elementary school teacher will need to
create a program for his students which can reinforce and supplement
the home situation. This program can include helping youngsters understand the roles of parents, the value of cooperation within the family, the
benefits of working together for common goals, the necessity of communicating feelings and attitudes, and the need for getting along with
other family members. Since the child's parents and siblings will constitute his image of family life, these must be considered in order to make
the school experience relevant to that life.

Suggested Activities

Career education may be hailed by educators as a breakthrough in
making education relevant to the lives of today's youth; however, without family and parental involvement, the objectives and goals of career
education can become isolated within the classroom, without becoming
an integral part of the life of the student. The effectiveness of the career
education movement may very well rest with the individual teacher's
ability to create a program that reaches out to the student not only in
the classroom but in all phases of the child's life. Teachers may glean
ideas from the following suggested activities, realizing that not every
program will work in a given area. These are only a few examples a wise
and innovative elementary teacher might devise to involve parents in
improving the contribution of home and family to career education.
With initiative and planning, teachers may create an effective program
for almost every situation.

Activity 1: Parents as Resources

Parents representing a broad base of careers make a classroom presentation illustrating aspects of their work. Wherever possible, actual
work situations are discussed, accompanied by pictures, uniforms, and
other paraphernalia characteristic of the field of work.

Teacher Involvement

(1) Become acquainted with the types of work performed by the parents.

(2) Contact those parents who represent a variety of careers to participate in the program.

(3) Orient parents on the purpose of the activity before the program is started.

(4) Prepare the students for the activity by making the necessary preparations to ensure that each parent, irrespective of his or her occupation, is treated with dignity and respect and that status is given to each career.

(5) Provide an experience whereby the children would list the contributions they feel the different occupations provide.

(6) Assist the students in understanding how many of these jobs relate to tasks in the home; for example, preparing meals and serving them (restaurant work), housecleaning (hotel management), grocery shopping (purchasing agent), paying bills (business management), repairing the car (auto mechanic), caring for the lawn and yard (landscaping).

(7) Conduct several follow-up activities (outlined below).

Follow-up Activities

Immediately following the activity, teachers should provide opportunities for students to become involved in learning about tasks related to the careers of their parents. For example, if a father is employed as a bus driver, let a student review the meaning and significance of traffic signals.

The teacher may wish to provide opportunities for the students to visit the worksite of one particular parent. For example, if a mother is a nurse, the class could visit a hospital (with the proper permission from the head of staff) so that the students could receive additional stimuli from an orientation on careers in the realm of medicine.

Activity 2: Parental Role-Playing by Students

(1) Assign all of the students to consult with their parents to learn of the kinds of work their parents perform in their occupations.

(2) Create sufficient ethusiasm and excitement in the classroom so that children will carry this feeling into the home.

(3) Encourage children to bring tools or wear clothing used by parents in connection with their work.

(4) Supervise practice sessions in the classroom.

(5) Invite parents to attend the classroom and participate in the activity.

(6) Supervise the activity in the classroom. If desired, the occupational exploration activity may be combined with music, drama, and art. For example:

  (a) In one elementary school in Atlanta, the students presented an "occupational operetta," writing the script and music and dramatizing the work their parents performed in their daily occupations. The operetta helped the parents as well as the children learn about the kinds of contributions all of the careers made to our society. This type of activity could be used to introduce or to climax a career exploration program.

  (b) In still another elementary school in Atlanta, the career exploration activity was combined with the fine arts area of education, with the children "interviewing" and then writing about the careers of their parents. In addition, the poet laureate of Georgia wrote poems about her impressions of the parents' jobs. As a follow-up, students also composed poems and sonnets, but these they sent to the poet laureate. The interchange of ideas and impressions was beneficial to students, parents, and perhaps even to the poet laureate.

Follow-up Activities

Teachers will find that the following activities will help to "cement" the new knowledge the students have about their parents' occupations:

(1) Review the various occupations that were acted out (or where applicable, were dramatized), and discuss the contributions of each career.

(2) Collect pictures of occupations that were not represented in the activity, and discuss their importance to the home and family living.

Activity 3: Consultations with Parents

Teachers should give ample time for consulting with parents to discuss career education and its implications and for counseling parents on relating home situations to those of the elementary school. Through parent-teacher conferences, consultations, organizations, meetings, or newsletters, the teacher can identify or explain projects in career education while soliciting parental help. Each teacher will need to select the manner in which it is most effective to contact parents within his local setting.

Teacher Involvement

(1) Organize and carefully plan conferences to identify projects and activities that will be discussed.

(2) Communicate personally with parents, offering them suggestions on how they can incorporate career exploration activities with home life. Point out how many work areas in the home relate to occupations outside the home.

(3) Listen to suggestions of parents and incorporate these into school activities wherever possible.

(4) Express enthusiasm for programs in career exploration in the home. Create an atmosphere in which parents will feel comfortable.

(5) Provide information to parents on the interests or abilities of their children. If parents seem to have unrealistic goals for their children, do not openly oppose their plans, but help them rechannel their thinking by pointing out abilities of their children in other endeavors.

(6) Conduct follow-up activities.

Activity 4: Exploring Work with Parents

The objective of this activity is to provide an opportunity for the child to observe his parent(s) on the job for a short period of time. First-hand knowledge of work at a factory, in a store or office, or at an outdoor worksite will give children an overview of their parents' niches in the world of work. The children will have a greater respect for the jobs and an appreciation of what the jobs entail, and will be better able to see how their parents relate to co-workers. The teacher can lay the foundation for accomplishing this activity by:

(1) After becoming acquainted with the work situations of the parents, plan a job visitation program that is practicable for local situations, selecting a committee of parents to assist in planning and implementing the activity. (See step 3 for examples.)

(2) Explain in detail to the students what this activity will entail: parents' approval, foreman's or supervisor's approval, etc. Generate enough enthusiasm in the children that they will be successful in securing participation of their parents.

(3) Work with the committee of parents in orienting all parents on the purpose of this activity. For this activity to be successful, the parents should understand at the outset that their efforts in securing permission for their children to visit them on the job will help to reinforce their children's concept of the workaday world. By having the various tasks explained to them, the youngsters will get a first-hand knowledge of the types of careers their parents are pursuing. For example:

   (a) A father or mother who is a barber or beauty shop operator might arrange for his or her son or daughter to visit the barber shop or beauty salon to see hair trimmed or cut: for a man, for a woman, for an older person, for a teenager, or for a child. The parent could expand the significance of the lesson by explaining the "psychology" he or she uses on the different customers in urging them to try a new hair style or a new tint. The parent could explain how barbering depends more on one's ability to sell people a service and make them pleased with the result than merely the cutting of hair. The children could relate this work with school lessons in mathematics (costs of various cuts, overhead, paying for supplies), social studies (explaining to customers how hair styles change), English (using proper grammar), and so forth.

(b) A retail sales clerk (mother or father) could arrange for the child to watch during the actual selling of an item, taking the money for the item sold, ringing the money on the cash register, "making change," bagging or wrapping the article, and thanking the customer as the parcel is presented. If the children visit at a time when there are no customers, they will see the parent keeping busy by arranging merchandise for display, stamping canned goods, marking price tags, and so forth. Any actual hands-on experience can provide the stimulus for a child to begin to think about the world of work, especially if the parent tells why he or she "likes" the job.

Parental Involvement

Several parents could become a working committee to plan activities — making arrangements for all of the children in the classroom to visit worksites, irrespective of the home environment. The ideal situation of course would be for all of the parents to participate by arranging for visitation to their jobs; but since this will be the exception rather than the rule, the committee could identify those whose employers accede to the request.

Activity 5: Learning to Manage

Through a role-playing activity in the classroom, the teacher can assist the children in learning how to purchase items for family use. The children could collect pictures from catalogs or magazines, determine the price they deemed appropriate for each item, and make price tags for the "merchandise." Then by using "play" money from a game or some they have made themselves, they could set up store and buy and sell the articles (pictures). As an extension of this activity, the children could take the money and pictures home and conduct a similar activity among family members.

Teacher Involvement

(1) Review the role of the family in buying goods and services.

(2) Provide the impetus for the children to bring play money and pictures of various types of merchandise (both expensive and inexpensive) to the classroom. Help them attach price tags to the items.

(3) Explain the buying and selling principles, and supervise the activity.

(4) Prepare a simple list of instructions for the children to take to their parents along with the play money and pictures so that the parents can reinforce the knowledge gained from this activity by engaging in a similar exercise at home.

(5) Conduct follow-up activities.

Parental Involvement

The parents may wish to make the home activity more personal and meaningful for their child by using actual buying and selling experiences and explaining them to the child — itemizing and tallying the cash register check tab from the grocery or dry goods store, comparing real bills and coins with those the child made in the classroom, checking costs of items in newspapers, catalogs, or magazines. Consulting the instruction checklist that the teacher prepared will make it easier for the parents to "zero in" on the specific areas of learning that their children are receiving in school.

Follow-up Activities

Devote several days to allowing the children to report on the buying and selling activities that were completed in their homes.

Activity 6: Who Am I?

This activity may become the most popular one in the school year: giving the child the opportunity to tell of the talents and abilities of family members. By outlining a "questionnaire" for the child to take home for interviewing family members, the teacher can guide the child in the rudiments of querying a person for information. Let the children help with the outline, incorporating good as well as not-so-good suggestions, but making sure that all suggestions are received with equal consideration.

Teacher Involvement

The teacher must be cognizant of various facets of psychology in this exercise, relying on his educated guesses as to whether a child shows an affinity for any activities below:

(1) As each child recites the talents, etc., of his or her family, be alert to any likes, dislikes, abilities, and interests that the child may display. Jot them down by each child's name so that you can relay them to the parents during consultations.

(2) Assist the students in preparing a handbook for recording special interests and goals.

(3) Assist the students in filling out a part of the handbook in the classroom.

(4) Encourage the students to take their handbooks home with them to discuss them with the family. A section should be filled in by each family member, with family goals set for each member.

Parental Involvement

The parents should review the handbook with their child, being alert for any special interests or abilities exhibited by themselves as well as the children. They can assist their children in setting goals and determining what must be done to achieve these goals.

Follow-up Activities

Teachers should review the handbooks with the students from time to time, encouraging the boys and girls to continue to add to the pages. The teachers can also encourage the students to engage in other activities outside the home and school which correspond to family and individual interests and abilities — churches, neighborhood theater groups, and the like.

SUMMARY

The home environment is the foundation for the development of fundamental values, attitudes, and skills which are the central factors of career success. The influence of the school and society on the child is infinitesimal in comparison to the home influence during the first five to eight years of life. If a child has had an unfortunate beginning, he can have attitudes altered; but this is a process that could take a lifetime.

Society's future depends upon widespread recognition that parenthood and successful homemaking must remain the underlying career roles for men and women producing the greatest satisfaction. *Successful* parenthood is not a natural instinct. It must be learned; therefore it can be taught.

The home environment is the most central factor in the development of basic values, attitudes, and basic skills which are the foundations of career success. All of the school's influence and that of society outside the home will never satisfactorily offset a bad home start. Parents are also the key educational decision makers whose support or lack of support will determine career education's future.

All children will have a career whether they are bright or dull, impoverished or richly endowed. The discovery of the career occurs in a developmental process of life-long duration, but the habits of discovery are formed in the childhood years. It is important that there be an alliance of elementary school teachers and parents at that critical time.

Suggestions for Further Reading

Bell, T. H. *Your Child's Intellect.* Salt Lake City: Olympus Publishing Company, 1972.

Breckenridge, Marian E.; and Vincent, E. Lee. *Child Development.* Philadelphia: W. B. Saunders Company, 1966.

Brigham Young University, Educational and Career Advisement Center. "Survey of Parent and Youth Attitudes in Career Guidance." Provo, Utah.

Bruner, Jerome S. *Research Program on Intellectual Development.* Cambridge, Massachusetts: Harvard University Press, 1965.

Englemann, Siegfried; and Engelmann, Therese. *Give Your Child a Superior Mind.* New York: Simon and Schuster, 1966.

Grant, Eva H. *Parents and Teachers as Partners.* Chicago: Science Research Associates, Inc., 1971.

Hayakawa, S. I. "On the Other Hand." *Saturday Evening Post* (Spring 1972).

Hopson, Barrie; and Hayes, John. *The Theory and Practice of Vocational Guidance.* Oxford: Pergamon Press, 1968.

Hoyt, Kenneth B.; Evans, Rupert N.; Mackin, Edward F.; and Mangum, Garth L. *Career Education: What It is and How to Do It.* Salt Lake City: Olympus Publishing Company, 1972.

McQueen, Mildred. "Parent Guidance and Education," Part 1, and "Involving Parents," Part 2, of *Ideas and Projects.* Science Research Associates (November 1972).

Sinick, Daniel. *You and Your Child's Career.* B'nai B'rith Vocational Service, 1966.

Smallenburg, Carol; and Smallenburg, Harry. "School Behavior — Whose Problem?" *PTA Magazine* (February 1971).

Williamson, E. G. *Vocational Counseling.* New York: McGraw-Hill Book Company, 1965.

6

Preservice and In-Service Training for Elementary School Teachers

As a set of concepts new to the experience of most classroom teachers and almost totally foreign to the training provided prospective teachers in most colleges of education, career education can expect to make little progress without a major reform of preservice teacher education practices and a massive in-service training effort. The examples given in the various chapters of this book may give the appearance of major change in U.S. education. But they represent only a small fraction of schools and a minority of teachers in those schools. Most practitioners of career education, few as they are, have progressed only to showing the career relevance of academic subject matter and to using a few classroom visitors and field trips. Real integration of the academic and the occupational is rare, and the use of the community as a learning environment is even more so. Teachers must both want to and know how to provide career education. This chapter suggests some of the teacher training needs and describes examples of steps toward such reforms. The suggestions and examples are substantive. The greater problem, gaining the commitment and finance for reform, is discussed in chapter 7.

PRESERVICE TEACHER TRAINING

Teacher-educators enjoy the comfortable monopoly position of being able to define the qualifications of a teacher and decreeing that none can teach without meeting those qualifications. They are in a position not only to control the supply of future instructors (which they have not done) and the content of their training (which they have done), but can also insist upon standards of competence which they themselves once had to meet. They validate the survival of their own teacher training institution so long as their sole function is to perpetuate these standards in new teachers, or to create still more teacher-educators. Given that unencroachable position, change in education can be incredibly slow without their endorsement and the involvement of the institutions in which they reside. Yet because they rarely confront the consumer demand which is the purview of the local district boards of education, they have little reason to change.

In the more stereotyped teacher training institutions, a devotion to the dissemination of content and theory has become dependent upon a summing of quarters, semesters, or trimesters which equate recitation and residence with teaching readiness. The "shiny new tools" which characterize a majority of teacher education programs command the neophyte's attention until he is released to his first raw, practice teaching experience in his third or final year of baccalaureate study. Thrust then from the controlled temperature of the clinical classroom on campus, this individual is forced to ground his entire commitment to a field on the basis of a single episode lasting from six to nine weeks. The dangers here are obvious. The combined perceptions of supervisor and internist are focused upon a critical incident sample alone, through which the potentially "good" teacher could be lost to the profession and the potentially fair (or "non" teacher), duped by one success, could become a liability to it.

These generalizations are harsh, but most schools which educate teachers have followed one of two basic models supporting them. State-supported institutions proclaim their need to adhere to that state's teacher certification requirements and rarely investigate alternatives in meeting or changing those requirements. Small, private, or research-based institutions present a management prototype equipping executive-level professionals or developing new materials and media for classroom use. Neither of these models questions the operating premise that teacher preparation is a historical constant based on fixed ratios of content to time.

Because of this placidity, these institutions can and have effectively resisted the sound of turbulence and change arising from their major consumers, the schools. When these voices are occasionally recognized, acknowledgment of this consumer trauma typically resolves in the institution's adding new course requirements or electives. Although these attempt to reflect topical concerns through the provision of urban and ethnic studies, group dynamics, or sensitivity training, the basic curriculum for preparation remains essentially the same. In sum, this smorgasbord of trend and issue offerings appears and disappears too rapidly for the eager novitiate and his adviser to be able to construct a program around them, while traditional demands continue to maintain their priority.

Those who elect to teach find themselves faced, as does the embryo physician, with the responsibility for acquiring expertise in a new methodology. More often than the physician, teachers must absorb the obsolete as well as the practicable in a program which rarely differentiates one from the other. Doctors can record from experience that "x" does not cure "y," and thus erase that nostrum from the required repertoires of future generations of doctors. Engineers and scientists neither fear nor suffer condemnation when theories fail the test of practice and no longer consume space in classroom and in text. The future teacher rarely has such surgery performed upon his course of study.

It is peculiar to the faith of the majority of teacher education programs that future practitioners not be burdened by evidence provided by their colleagues in the field. Presenting all educational forms ever conceived as having utility, it is also an article of faith that this burdensome portfolio will somehow achieve the transformation of the student into the master teacher. The new teacher enters the classroom convinced that knowledge and methodology alone will more than compensate for the discrepancies he sees between the clinical norm and the learning styles of his students. It is a conviction that is quickly invalidated. Now on the firing line, the new teacher finds that no college classroom prepared him to be innovative, flexible, or more than verbally receptive to differing cultures and values. Those gifts, if he has them, had been acquired and were maintained in spite of, not because of, his training program.

Reforming Teacher Education

This indictment is by no means universal. Some who prepare teachers are recognizing that in order to motivate students to become autonomous learners and to support them as they develop alternative responses and decision-making skills, future practitioners need first to demonstrate a mastery of these behaviors themselves. The Carnegie Commission on Higher Education has advocated the development of performance-based criteria throughout universities which would permit the student to "stop out" at certain well-defined junctures; to obtain his credentials in three years or less, or to demonstrate college-level competence without ever having been formally enrolled in a college or university. But though these ideas are being studied and tried in institutions of higher education across the nation, no more than a handful of teacher training institutions are similarly engaged. Meantime, more radical approaches advocate bypassing the teacher education function for direct access to the educational and social milieu of the public schools. These changes are illustrated by an increased number of field research projects, active contract/voucher systems established between university and community, and merger of discrete departments and discipline areas into amalgams of "learning environments," "public psychology," and "human development."

The few efforts to restructure teacher education such as those connected with the Center for Teaching and Learning at the University of South Dakota and Michigan State's Elementary Education majors[1] exemplify what teacher education might be, given time and resources. The ill-concealed impatience of the school as a knowledgeable consumer, combined with the reluctance of the U.S. Office of Education to invest more than token funds in teacher training programs, conspires to delay a thoughtful investigation of potential reforms.

Few would argue with Etzioni's premise that it is more difficult to change people than it is to change their surroundings.[2] To spend time and funds in changing the value systems of college professors is a futile

---

[1] Taken from the University of South Dakota's New School of Behavioral Studies in Education, from Michigan State University's An Experiment in Elementary Teacher Education, and from the Training of Teachers, Eastern High School, Lansing, Michigan.

[2] Anatole Etzioni, "Human Beings Are Not so Easy to Change After All," *Saturday Review* (April 3, 1972).

exercise. Direct involvement of professor and prospective teacher in the realities of community and classroom is more effective. However fixed a professorial value, no attitude or perception could go unchanged for long — given repeated blows by hard experience. His student, the future teacher, would have an admitted advantage here. While equally buffeted, he would become acclimated to truth by virtue of his early and continuing exposure throughout his training experience. If it repelled him, he would learn something about himself soon enough to seek out alternate ways to accomplish his people-oriented mission. If it challenged him, the profession's body of knowledge could assume a particular and purposeful dimension as he becomes increasingly adept in relating its content to the needs of those who will populate his future work setting.

Suggestions for In-Service Training

This chapter offers examples of innovative practices emanating from the task of preparing teachers to practice career education which might serve as impetus for those who prepare teachers to teach. Unfortunately, most of these examples issue from other departments than colleges of education, or from the forward-looking programs being developed by certain community colleges. It may be useful to parallel these practices with specific recommendations which could have implications for those who set teacher certification standards — with the hope that their reexamination of those standards would motivate a simultaneous effort at the university level.

Innovative Programs

The University of Wisconsin, Green Bay, has focused its entire four-year program on environmental problems. All discipline areas are teamed with community work settings where students apply scientific and social principles to the prevention as well as the remediation of an inbalance of natural resources. Communication be-

Recommendations for Teacher Training

Develop a training sequence which recognizes a predetermined community characteristic (farming, resort area, heavy industry), a community resource (preponderance of "retired" workers), or a well-articulated community concern (unemployment, ecology, ethnic inequity). Relate acquisition of teaching methodology to

tween faculty, students, and townspeople has led to a sociological involvement extending far beyond the initial topic of ecology.

Ferris State College in Big Rapids, Michigan, has responded to a marked change in the stated objectives of its predominantly white, middle-class student body — by offering associate degrees in automobile repair and autobody mechanics, among others. The step-in/step-out flexibility of the program has permitted students to test alternatives while becoming economically independent.

Evergreen State College in Olympia, Washington, encourages beginning students to contract with faculty on courses to study. One group agreed to design a municipal park for a nearby city. Judgment of competency is based on agreement between recipient's evaluation of the service rendered and the student's self-assessment.

Prairie State College in Chicago Heights, Illinois, offers an associate degree program to students who wish employment in preschool situations, day-care centers, hospital playrooms, and nurseries. Early work experience assists students to set alternate goals,

curriculum reflecting any or all of these consumer realities.

Establish a continuing registration option for those students who plan for income-producing experiences which appear to conflict with initially expressed goals. Apply the dynamics of these experiences to the restructuring of the internship phase in such a way that alternate future school resource roles can be considered.

Accommodate faculty/student contracts for off-campus involvements which result directly or indirectly in school-community benefit. Assess increased or decreased willingness of student to eventually confront a classroom situation after a mutually established quota of peripheral experiences has been undertaken.

Develop a phase one exploratory experience which serves as reality-testing for men and women who declare elementary school teaching as majors. During the final semester of the freshman year, assign them to local agencies, hospitals, and private day-

Innovative Programs

Recommendations for
Teacher Training

based on tested ability in the field of child care.

care centers as volunteer aides for two afternoons a week. In the sophomore year, place students in schools, in school board offices, and in state education departments for a minimum of three 2-week internships.

St. Mary's Junior College in Minneapolis offers a two-year program in child development technology, with emphasis upon the special skills needed by assistants to special education programs. Early clinical and field experiences determine student receptivity to the exceptional child.

Permit immediate access and apprenticeship to an experienced practitioner in either school, institution, or hospital to students declaring special education as their interest. Provide frequent opportunity for discussion with parents of exceptional children. Refrain from imposing disproportionate coursework and theory until the ambience of the specialization is demonstrably clear to the student.

Florida Junior College in Jacksonville and State University of New York in Cobleskill are two of an increasing number of institutions offering A.A. degrees in hotel/motel management. These offer options in areas of institutional food and restaurant management, as well as coursework in the psychological dynamics of the "organization" dealing with leisure and personal services.

Provide course options which can both prepare and expose students who wish to become school administrators through intensified undergraduate exposure to organizational psychology. Increasingly sophisticated skills could be acquired (or credited through past experience) through residency in industrial personnel departments, business and office firms, and summer camp or resort motel experiences.

Montgomery College in Rockville, Maryland, and North Hen-

Establish minimum requirements of community apprentice-

nepin State Junior College in ship to the college or university Brooklyn Park, Minnesota, offer town's local government. This programs in urban planning and could enable the future teacher to development. Graduating tech-assess his tolerance of, and poten-nicians become neighborhood om-tial contribution to yet another budsmen, as well as expert assis-establishment - based institution tants to the city "fathers," who which is and will be directly re-must achieve balance between the lated to his future teaching role. social, physical, and economic realities of their communities.

The University of Nevada in Create an "education" major Las Vegas has declared that en-which does not demand premature tering students no longer need to declarations by students of future declare an academic "major." Ex-grade, content, or age-level associ-ploration of various interdisciplin-ations. Through the combination ary programs and removal of time of some of the options described limits for course completion re-above, determine with the stu-focus curriculum on student needs dent where and with whom his and interests. "known" skills will achieve their maximum exercise at an arbitrary point late in his sophomore year.

A nationally eminent, state school officer has said that we "once looked to the colleges of education for leadership in innovation," adding that they are now "among the major obstacles to change." Though this may be an excessively harsh generalization, it is evident that the demands to which career education responds arise for government, employers, the community in general, and from public school educators, but rarely from the teacher training institutions. But the ultimate consumer of the product of teacher education is that broader community which can ulti-mately make its demands felt.

The Impact of Teacher Surplus

The cutback in elementary teacher preparation, responsive to declin-ing overall demand after fifteen years of falling birth rates may suggest a diminution of input from new teachers and limitations to the reform of teaching practices through preservice training. True in the aggregate, the situation is more promising in the specific.

There remain teacher shortages in certain geographic areas — inner cities and rural communities — and in certain fields — special education, bilingual education, industrial and home arts, and vocational education. Men are in high demand in the early as well as the intermediate elementary grades. Highly motivated and trained young people are being sought by communities of heavy minority populations. Women will find that school options are not limited to teaching and counseling alone; they include a range of careers, from the discretely trained paraprofessional to the resource specialist in career education who serves both school and community.

Less visible, but at the heart of this thesis, are the very real opportunities for elementary school teachers who come to the school experience equipped to plan as well as teach, to write curricula responsive to the world the child must enter, and to conduct or participate in staff development experiences which reflect their own first-hand knowledge of a variety of noneducational settings. Institutions preparing teachers can now choose from a number of viable alternatives which can reengage the interest and enthusiasm of their students while coming to terms with the not inconsistent "qualifiers" for federal largesse. With the knowledge that the U.S. Office of Education has a better-than-chance record for assessing and responding to public consensus, such institutions cannot afford to dismiss out of hand an opportunity to validate their existence. A slow-up in the persistent demand for new teachers should both allow and force teacher education institutions to reexamine their product and their practices. It is a buyer's market now, and the schools should refuse both to accept the ill-prepared and to "buy" from institutions not meeting the needs of the market. The following set of questions, which have been rephrased from the original,[3] might be a useful assessment of the willingness of a college of education to meet those needs.

(1) Does the teacher education program permit and produce dialogue with other disciplines and outside organizations?

---

[3] Adapted from Walter S. Mietus, "Industrial Arts Teacher Education in the Age of Industrial Obsolescence," paper presented to the American Industrial Arts Association's 33d Annual Convention, April 22, 1971, in Miami, Florida, and from Christopher Sower, *The Normative Sponsorship Theory of Updating Organizations* (East Lansing, Michigan: Michigan State University, 1968).

(a) Is there evidence of requests from these agencies to use materials, facilities, and academic talents of teaching personnel?

(b) Is there evidence of planned teacher-educator exchange with inhabitants of other work settings which exceed traditional short-term consulting roles?

(c) Is there evidence of cross-disciplinary unity in the establishment of institutional goals which respond to the consumer school systems' analysis of need and thereby to the reality of teacher placement?

(2) Does the press describe the program as being useful to society in terms of its image to the taxpayer, to the legislator, and to the elected or appointed state board of education?

(a) Is there evidence that the individual parent and businessman considers his investment in teacher education a sound one; e.g., the citizenry's reaction to bond issues, tuition increases, teacher unemployment, and conflicting public school-based issues?

(b) Is there evidence of legislative involvement and support for programs requiring additional funds to prepare teachers in new ways; e.g., do memories of new obsolescent programs dilute enthusiasm?

(c) Is there evidence of responsiveness between state boards and departments of education and the long-range plans of teacher training institutions?

(3) Does the program use a maximum amount of human energy directed toward goal achievement and a minimum amount to maintenance functions and contesting behaviors?

(a) Is there evidence of a wide use of community and industrial teaching and setting resource during the preservice experience?

(b) Is there evidence that the program equips teachers to accept and deal with differing cultures and values through direct contact with those espousing them?

(c) Is there evidence that teacher training sequences study and employ the public school systems' in-service and staff development procedures as models for preservice variation?

(4) Does the program have the ability to attract and hold the loyalty of young and competent applicants?

(a) Is there evidence of consistency between the presentation of a number of learning theories and the flexibility of faculty in accommodating differing learning styles and motivations of future teachers?

(b) Is there evidence of accommodation of varying goals, declared uncertainties, mistrials, and radical theory in the exploratory stage engaged by all students?

(c) Is there evidence of curricular reflection of faculty growth and faculty commitment to the social/educational milieu reported by his reality-oriented student?

And the final, more verifiable question: How many students who are declared qualified to teach actually enter and stay in the teaching profession? This and the preceding questions could serve as genesis for the positive confrontation between those who educate the school practitioner and the child and society they are expected to serve.

IN-SERVICE TEACHER TRAINING

No matter what is done to improve the quality and the career education orientation of new entrants to the profession, educational reforms for a long time to come will depend upon refurbishing those already committed to educational careers. More has been accomplished and less has been written in the area of staff development than any other single educational dimension. Here, as in every trade or profession, internal efforts to upgrade the practitioner's skills receive little publicity and only faint praise from the paternal colleges of education . . . while a mystified public wonders what all those teachers could be doing during childless school days and long summers.

With the advent of career education, in-service summer work sessions are beginning to assume a corporate status equal to, if not surpassing the triannual pilgrimage to the nearest accrediting institution. Moreover, in a few progressive locations, the private citizen is not only becoming aware of what is going on, but is often involved in ways which influence the educational "establishment."

In-service has become career education's most articulate spokesman, from state education departments to individual school districts. The ambiguity once associated with the educator's periodic self-examination has been transformed into a purposeful investigation of an institutional and personal capacity for change. Much of the enthusiasm can be attributed to career education's high visibility, but even more credit must be given to a dynamic which permits the educator to save face by losing it. Through his embrace of new human expertise, he is able to maintain his orientation role while relinquishing his exclusive claim to educative superiority. Since there is no imposition of a "third party" edict, but rather a task that each has similarly defined as having to be done, the teacher and the community representative are eyeball to eyeball in a learning situation which places them both, with equal "handicaps," on the starting line.

Staff development procedures vary from state to state and from school to school, but common elements can be extracted from these approaches which have achieved effective implementation of career awareness programs in the elementary school. While some of these practices are and were attendant upon proposals submitted for funding (and thereby more subject to attrition), the majority of exemplary in-service models have been developmentally generated by state education departments and school districts which predicted career education's currency long before its arrival as a national priority. Another distinguishing feature of these more enduring models is the continuing support they receive from their state boards, and often their state governments. While this support is not always geared to the provision of unlimited funds, it is marked by the extremely good press associated with public commitments by individuals or institutions who can either influence or establish long-range educational policy.

Career education in-service patterns can be said to fall into eight categories. A brief description of each might serve to illustrate certain options which have attained staff objectives for those who chose to implement them.

Each of the approaches and the specific elements described are realities in many states and local subdivisions. A combination of any or all of these in-service practices could become a continuing orchestration of staff development procedures for school systems implementing effective and enduring career education programs. While there has been no attempt to arrange the sample approaches in order of initiation — for many can and do occur simultaneously with good effect — the reality of human and material investment and maintenance demands attention to an orderly sequence of planning which continually rewards the practitioner in other than extrinsic ways. This encouragement is the good "press," both internal to the profession and external to the public, which serves to reinforce a growing cadre of career education experts while it ensures increasing excellence in programs for their children.

The Working Sabbatical Approach

A given school system elects to release *x* number of school personnel from all disciplines, kindergarten through twelfth grade (K–12), for *y* number of school terms. Financial outlay is required to restaff vacancies, to maintain full pay for researching teachers, and to provide the minimum clerical and "materials" assistance needed. *The charge:* to survey both the literature on, and the live example of career education in practice — thus to create curricula linking each subject matter area to an operational definition of its application to a worker's life-style. *The test:* to concurrently select a pilot system, K–12, in which to test developed curriculum, and another, closely matched system which could serve as a control. *The implementation:* to move certain members of the researching team into the pilot setting to serve as resource to staff while training them in the use of the new materials and approaches.

The Planned Summer Work Experience Approach

A pilot school continuum, K–12, contracts with a number of local businesses representing nine broad career areas (environmental, agri-business, health, real estate/banking/finance, personal services, public services, communications, manufacturing, construction, and transportation) to provide up to eight weeks of full-time employment for two teachers from each grade level (total, 26) during the summer months. Employers assign one worker to each teacher as an "advocate." The school district bears all costs in year 1 by extending ten-month salaries into a twelve-month category. The state education departments arrange with a local college or university to bear the cost of tuition "credit" for worker advocates, while working teachers pay the usual tuition fees to obtain graduate credit for their paid summer experience.

In each succeeding year, increasing numbers of teachers have this exposure with a proportionate increase in the employer's financial contribution (and a proportionate decrease in the school district's subsidy) issuing from the employer's perception of the program's value and the teachers' work performance. The college or university continues to award credit, or to provide "rain checks" for course work in guidance to those advocates assigned to teachers.

The Intensive Summer Workshop Approach

State education department personnel conduct consecutive workshops for teachers, counselors, administrators, content area supervisors, and directors of curriculum, guidance, and vocational education. These are held at local area colleges for graduate credit or at "neutral" sites for state education department professional credit. As part of the state's plan for orientation to and implementation of career education practices, K–adult, consultant and resource material costs are minimized by wide use of local citizenry from the "workshop" community.

Housing fees and graduate tuition are borne by state education department funds allocated for staff and program standards development (two categories combined) under the state's plan for career education. Workshop products are twofold: a cadre of professionals are trained to conduct in-service, and beginning outlines of local curriculum guides with accompanying implementation time tables are constructed.

The Assured Released Time for Planning Approach

School systems initiate flexible scheduling, permitting two hours weekly in which school "teams" (department heads, counselors, administrators, etc.) can meet with rotating faculty groups. These sessions are used to plan for the most effective implementation of those curriculum activities generated through prior workshop experiences. Faculty not involved in particular planning sessions contribute to the regularity of this released time by taking part in those field trips, outdoor projects, or large assemblies which are components of the school's career awareness program. In addition, the administrative policy for substitutes is adjusted to recognize and use the experts in the community as spokesmen and demonstrators of a wide variety of careers during those times when planning sessions are taking place.

The Year-Long Industry-Visitation Approach

A state education department contracts with local colleges or universities to award credits on a graduating scale to teachers and counselors who attend some or all industry visitations scheduled monthly during the school year. These visits are arranged by large businesses, industries, or agencies in a centrally located metropolitan area in the state, at no cost to the participants except their own travel to that area. The investment made by industry is considered well spent when teachers and counselors return to their schools with new information and understanding about the continuing human needs required to maintain and improve products and services. Each visit is either concluded or introduced by a seminar in which participants have the opportunity to question the man on the line, as well as his personnel management representative.

The Addition of Resource Staff Approach

School districts which have allocated funds for staff increase consider the option of training and employing paraprofessionals to assist with the implementation of career education programs. Alternatively, they might elect to submit proposals to their state funding agencies for these personnel. In both cases, such assistance is directed toward a valid career education resource function in the school system. Some examples of these are:

(1) Additional pay for teachers with industrial experience who serve in pre- and post-school hour capacity as school-business community liaison; or salary for a retired member of the working community who holds a similar position during school hours.

(2) Employment of interested high school-aged youth as instructional aides, tutors, remedial specialists, and media specialists. These young people could be enrollees in a cooperative work experience program, unemployed school dropouts, or between decisions to seek further education, training, or work. As "living witnesses" to brief work or nonwork experiences (in terms of their current perceptions of the basic skills they did or did not acquire during the elementary school years), they share with young students a glimpse of the future in store for them.

(3) Employment of instruction aides for teachers at each grade level. These individuals are drawn from the parent, retired, and unemployed communities around the school and are involved in the in-service and planning process with the teachers.

The Serial, or State Board to State Education Department to Regional Approach

For some states, the most effective approach has been for educators to secure the leadership of the governor — in appointing experts to conduct a one-day "lay" conference introducing the rationale and concept of career education to representatives of the business-labor-industry community. Immediately following this event, the state department of education conducts a professional conference for its line staff in all subdivisions. On this occasion, exemplary practices already in existence are displayed in one setting. This achieves recognition for the practitioners and prototype and consolidation for those at district level. Both of these activities are dependent upon the state board of education's support of career education as a statewide educational priority, and its commitment, often by resolution, to the implementation of that priority in its school systems.

After receiving evaluation and recommendation from both groups of participants, the state education department and its colleague state citizens advisory committee assist with the state's regional in-service meetings which follow. These serve to develop regional strength for future local leadership with in-service functions. Ultimately the local school, having been given the assurance of known educational policy and human (if not financial) support, is able to bring its own talents to bear on a customized school-wide plan which is also consonant with the goals of its own subdivision and its state plan for career education.

The Project or Interdisciplinary Approach

Subsequent to the investigation and groundwork by district level content area supervisors (in forms of curriculum outlines, position papers, etc.), local schools initiate an interdisciplinary team on their premises. Using the released time for planning they are assured, they commit themselves to the use of a "project," "interest," or "task" approach to curriculum design. The sequence of activities planned for each school year evolves from the team's considered assessment of the readiness and interest levels of their students and are designed to involve youngsters from all grade levels in varying and appropriate ways.

In each of these long-term ventures, the necessity of competency in each subject area would be emphasized as key to the successful completion of that work simulation activity. Some examples from actual practices are:

(1) Environmental "engineering" around the school

(2) Boutiques, garden-markets, four-season products

(3) Bakery adjuncts to the school's cafeteria

(4) School "employment" service

(5) Public address system, film, slide, and video tape-recorder productions

(6) Peer tutoring and "brother/sister" counseling

(7) Newspapers, student-built illustrated story and textbooks for younger schoolmates

(8) Drama, dance, and music productions

(9) Human ecology: diet, hygiene, social studies, junior olympics

Adapting In-Service Experiences

As stressed in chapter 2, the teacher must be involved in the process of developing creative career education experiences and integrate the teaching of their academic subjects in the way that suits them; so must school districts design their own in-service programs. Also counselors, teachers, and administrators intent upon changing their training programs to include skills of integrating career education into each of these levels must design their own programs. Career education integration must begin with the teachers who are already teaching before training institutions will seriously consider including it in their training programs.

Any school district which wishes to change teaching practices must work with people who are willing to change at the administrative, counseling, and teacher levels. If an administrator wants to move into career education and the teachers are not ready, no amount of coercion will provide a relevant program. On the other hand, teachers who wish to integrate career education into their teaching practices will soon be stymied with red tape if the administrator is not supportive. A counselor's feeling about the program is yet another gauge on which to predict its success.

Since administrative support and counselor (if there is one) support are important, anyone who seeks to become a change agent should begin at this level. These two groups must first understand what career education is. This is best accomplished through an informal meeting where all aspects of the program are clearly defined. Administrators and counselors should be allowed to ask questions and react during this meeting.

After this has been accomplished, those administrator-counselor teams who are interested in the program should *volunteer* to have their entire staffs exposed to the same type of meeting. Then, those teachers who wish to take the risk to teach their subject matter in a different way will become involved in in-service training. From this evolves a very practicable team from the school which not only will work together, but will reinforce each other's efforts. The administrator and the counselor become completely involved in the in-service training.

A group of four or five teachers in a school is an ideally sized group. If there are more teachers involved, then two or more groups should be formed. Administrators who would like to get their entire staff involved can be reassured that in consecutive years, other groups of teachers will want their turn. Eventually, 80 to 90 percent of the staff will be teaching subject matter through the vehicle of career education.

In Sonoma County, California, a project beginning with six teachers in each of three schools mushroomed to 150 teachers in 15 schools, with 100 teachers and five schools on a waiting list for the following year. In this same county, the counselor education department of the local state college asked to be able to put counseling interns into the career education schools to train counselors to work with teaching staffs and community resources as part of their counseling role. Two other state colleges have also made contact to use the schools for interning purposes.

In a career education program which failed, compiled sets of career education activities were placed in a book and given to the other teachers for their use. These books were placed on the shelf by teachers; they had no involvement in their development and therefore had little motivation to use them. Those teachers who were involved in the writing could not understand why the other teachers were not excited about it. Many curriculum revisions have been stifled this way.

The key of course is that as teachers become involved in development, they grow excited about implementation. Yet few teachers will have the built-in initiative to undertake development of their own career education materials, unless that development occurs within a structured in-service training and curriculum development program. Even within such a structural program, many will lack the imagination to develop wholly new materials, but they can be helped and inspired to adapt materials that others have developed to the particular needs of their classrooms and students. There will be some teachers in each staff who may never get involved, yet pressure will not encourage these students to integrate career education into their curricula. In other words, career education involvement has a spiraling effect. It begins with a core of interested, energetic teachers and begins to widen out year after year until most of the teachers in the school can no longer avoid the excitement generated by the students of those teachers.

Another pitfall has occurred where programs have attempted to have teachers write terminal objectives before getting involved in the program. This had a stifling effect on teachers interested in career education. Although objectives are needed, these can best be prepared as the teachers are involved in the program. Objectives that are written up before any involvement in actual implementation are no more than a frustrating exercise.

A third pitfall occurs when administrators force teachers to become involved when they are not ready, or force them to provide without adaptations career education experiences that have been developed by someone else. It is necessary for school staffs to decide on a minimum number of experiences, but this is best done as a cooperative measure.

An in-service teaching program should be based on the educational need of the learners in the school district, the needs of the working communities surrounding these schools, and the creative endeavor of teachers, counselors, and administrators working together to initiate a program. The experts on which exploratory activities are appropriate for each grade level are the creative teachers in the classrooms. These teachers, working with someone to stimulate them to think about the world of work and to acquaint them with the resources available, can come up with the best program for their classrooms. Teachers, if provided the time, can create a career education program which is superior to any prepackaged plan in that it reflects the needs and resources of their communities and their students. Yet, since all teachers will not and cannot do this, it is useful to collect or develop tried career education learning experiences which can be adapted to particular needs.

Model for In-Service Training

The following model of in-service training is presented as a workable method used in some districts in California, Washington, Maryland, and New York.

A minimum of three days should be scheduled to thoroughly acquaint teachers with the group process itself. It is also suggested that a parent be included in each group for these in-service days. Parents not only can provide good creative ideas, but can also be used later to implement the experiences created. They also act as informational leaders for other parent groups.

Group process can be conducted from one day to five weeks (one-half days) to help each teacher work out plans to be implemented in the classroom, and also work out a role definition for the administrator, the counselor, and the parent in career education. If the school has paraprofessionals, they should also be involved in this group process. Alternatives to paid paraprofessionals will be discussed later in this chapter.

There are many activities that can be planned to provide career education experiences. Teachers generally think first of entire class field trip and speakers to come into the classroom. However, creative teachers have planned plays, pantomimes, role-playing exercises, bulletin board displays, collages, parent and business speakers, leisure-time demonstrations, charts, small investigative teams of students with cameras and recorders who then report to the entire class on what they have learned, mock interviews, value games, interest aptitude games, student reports, student interviews, student- and teacher-made media, art activities, and many others.

Teachers may initially have difficulty in getting started. Groups representing different grade levels are more creative and productive, and groups made up of men and women are more creative than those consisting of all women or all men. It is best for a leader to be appointed by the group.

Ten career education concepts, such as those listed in chapter 2, are suggested as a realistic number with which to work. If a school has several teams, they might meet at first as an entire group and decide upon a list of career education objectives for the entire school. Generally speaking, school objectives and classroom objectives are best established if a list of working concepts for the school is developed. The guideline for group leaders in the following section is suggested.

FORMAT FOR THE SCHOOL GROUP-PLANNING MEETING

Each group should include no more than five teachers and should contain both men and women.

1. Introduce resource person (five minutes).[4]

2. Choose a leader (someone from the school other than an administrator).

3. Read the concepts and choose one which appeals to the group for brainstorming session (ten minutes).

4. Brainstorming session (20 to 45 minutes). Begin to think of as many ways as possible to put the concept across to a group of children represented by the group (elementary, junior high, senior high). Do not have any constraints during this brainstorming session (money, time, etc.).

5. One teacher is to choose an idea and develop it into a total plan. Get down to details (thirty minutes).

   a. Which resource people to use.

   b. What could happen leading into the experience.

   c. What will follow.

   d. Objectives:

      (1) Relate verbal concepts of subject matter to concrete experience of world of work at the student level.

      (2) Increase knowledge: What do you expect students to know afterward that they didn't know before? Examples:

         (a) "Students will be able to name five skills an auto mechanic must have" (occupational information objective).

---

[4] The resource person in this case is a teacher who has already been involved in career education and can be of great help to a beginning group. This also reinforces the teacher's career education implementation skills and imparts new ideas.

(b) "Students will be able to make up five math prob-
    lems to give to the rest of the class that is typical of
    the math a nurse would need to know" (subject
    matter objective).

(c) "Students will write a paragraph of the leisure ac-
    tivities available for a person who works at night"
    (concept objective).

6. Next teacher develops a plan (thirty minutes). This may not be
   from the concept; it could be from a unit; could just be an idea;
   could be a friend with an interesting job or hobby. Eventually
   try to tie it into a concept.

7. Next teacher, etc. (thirty minutes each).

8. Help administrator define his role (thirty minutes).

9. Help counselor define his role (thirty minutes).

10. Help parent define his role.

An important planning stage is to help teachers realize that they have
creative potential. One workable way to effect this is by having the small
teams choose one concept and for 30 to 45 minutes "brainstorm" about
the many different ways in which they could put that concept across.
During this brainstorming period, constraints of time, money, etc.,
should be eliminated. Teams have found that they begin slowly but that
the stimuli of one idea produce other ideas in the group. Often very
creative ideas can be developed during this time.

After this initial brainstorming session, one of the teachers chooses
one idea that has been generated from the brainstorming session and
attempts to develop it into a well-thought-out career education learning
experience. All of the teachers will help this teacher develop this into a
workable plan. The following planning format has been helpful to
teachers in working out the learning experience.

FORMAT FOR EXPERIENCE PLANNING AND EVALUATION

1. Major concept supporting the learning outcome.

2. Preparation required (steps or discussions leading into experience).

3. Objectives to be met (concept, occupational information, and
   subject matter).

4. Describe the experience.

5. Resource people that were used.

6. What curriculum areas were incorporated into the experience, and how this was done?

7. Evaluation in terms of students' enthusiasm, success, or failure. (What percentage of students met objectives? Not to be assessed until completion of experience.)

8. What other concept or concepts were incorporated into the experience?

The evaluation section is naturally completed after the experience has been implemented. In the planning of an experience, teachers will eventually learn to include concept objectives, occupational information objectives, and subject matter objectives.

To illustrate the three types of objectives, the following examples are given:

(1) *Concept:* Leisure-time activities may influence career choice, and career choice may affect leisure-time activities.

(2) *Experience:* the teacher has students compile a list of questions to ask a nurse working at night and one working during the day. The teacher arranges a mock interview so that students will feel comfortable in interviewing procedures and will have specific questions to ask. A night nurse from a local hospital comes into a fourth grade class to talk about her job and her life-style. The next day a group of five students visits the hospital and talks to a nurse who works on the day shift, and interviews her on her job. They tape the interview with an inexpensive tape recorder and take slides with an inexpensive self-developing camera which shows the nurse doing different tasks. The students report to the class, show slides, and have the class listen to the recording. After the night nurse talks, a group of five are chosen to go to the hospital. They have specific tasks to perform:

(a) One student will choose ten spelling words necessary for the nurse to know.

(b) One student will learn to operate a tape recorder.

(c) One student will operate the camera.

　　　(d) One student will compile ten math problems illustrative of those used in nursing to give to the rest of the class.

　(3) Out of such a project, the following objectives should have been achieved:

　　　(a) Students will be able to name five skills necessary for a nurse (occupational information objective).

　　　(b) Each student will write a paragraph of the leisure activities available for a person who works at night vs one who works during the days (concept objective).

　　　(c) Students will work ten math problems related to nursing (subject matter objective: math).

　　　(d) Students will write a paragraph (subject matter objective: English).

　　　(e) Students will spell correctly ten words used in nursing (subject matter objective: spelling).

　The interview, the photography, and the recording could also be related to specific subject matter areas.

A creative teacher could relate many other subject areas to this experience. One enterprising elementary school teacher who had been a physical therapist worked out exercises for the physical education teacher which were related to jobs: the pole climbers, the shovelers, the lifters, etc.

Although creative ideas can be generated from a concept, there are other ways in which activities can be formed. For instance, a social studies class studying a western desert decided to find out about job opportunities available in the desert in comparison to those available on the Pacific Coast. Each student, looking at a map of the United States, chose a particular desert town. He then wrote to the chamber of commerce of that town and asked for a copy of the local newspaper. When the newspaper arrived, students compiled a list of the greatest demand jobs in each city. They then wrote for Coastal newspapers and did the same analysis. Although the idea generated from social studies, it is easy to see how other academic subjects could be related and how it could also relate to a concept. Here it was found that some career availability is limited in certain geographic locations.

It is easy to see how students could also gain occupational information by either writing to a person doing this job to ask certain questions or research it through some occupational books written for elementary schools. Therefore the following objectives could be met:

(1) Students will name five major jobs found in the desert which are not found on the Coast (subject matter objective: social studies. Also concept objective, since it is related to the concept).

(2) Students will choose one of those jobs and be able to name five skills necessary and one place where training could be received (occupational information objective).

(3) Students will write a letter to one desert or Coastal community (subject matter objective: writing, spelling, etc.).

(4) Students will compute ratios of jobs between Coast and desert (math).

Another way to derive an experience is just from knowing someone who the teacher thinks would make an interesting speaker. For example, one second grade teacher speeding to school was stopped by a motorcycle policeman. While he was writing the ticket for speeding, she was thinking that her second graders would be very interested in his motorcycle and uniform. She asked if he would be willing to speak to her class, and he agreed. She preceded his visit by discussing with her class what they thought a policeman did and recorded the discussion on tape. After setting up the appointment with the policeman, she asked him if there were other people who worked for the police department that could come also. What had been until that time an abstract concept — "Our society causes interrelationships of jobs" — was assuming concreteness.

The day after the discussion, the motorcycle policeman drove his "bike" into the classroom with lights flashing, and a patrol car pulled outside. A woman and a long-haired man from the narcotics division also came into the classroom. They talked briefly about their work and how, even though their jobs were different, they depended upon one another. Students were allowed to ask questions, use the two-way radios between the bike and patrol car, handle the handcuffs and other equipment, and try on the hats. (Because the students remarked that they felt differently when they wore the hard hat from the way they felt when wearing a soft hat, the teacher was motivated to develop another career education learning experience built around hats that represent different occupations.)

After one hour, the teacher served coffee to the visitors and had the students draw a picture about anything related to the police department. They also wrote a one-line sentence about one thing they had learned from the discussion. The members of the police force circulated around the room and helped them spell, etc.

Each student's drawing and sentence were displayed around the classroom. During one week, each student was given some time each day to learn to read other students' sentences. Spelling words were given from the sentences, and math was related to "policemen" terms. The objectives of this exercise were:

(1) Each student will be able to tell one way in which policemen help him and one way in which they help each other (concept objective).

(2) Each student will draw one picture and write a sentence about a policeman (subject matter objective: art, writing, reading, spelling).

(3) Each student will tell one thing a policeman does (occupational information objective).

After each teacher in the group has developed a career education learning experience, the other members of the group (parent, administrator, paraprofessional, student, counselor, etc.) attempt to define their role in relationship to each experience and also to the total career education program. The administrator may have some contacts related to district policy, the paraprofessional may have some equipment to arrange for, the parent may decide to initiate a program for the PTA on career education. Each person in the group has some responsibility for the program and his role should be clearly defined. Although his responsibility is his own definition, others in the group should contribute suggestions. Counselors have found that this has contributed to a role change for them which was more exciting and vital than previously.

An important key in designing a program is for teachers to realize that there is no one best way to implement career education. As the groups continue to work together and become accustomed to thinking along career education lines, they become more innovative and quicker to develop career-related experiences. (High school teachers sometimes have difficulty in working in groups because they have been alienated from other subject matter groups for most of their teaching lives.) Teachers at all levels, however, find this to be an exciting way of developing curriculum once they overcome their initial reticence. Several groups can work at one time and in the same room. It is possible for fifty staff members in teams of four or five to work in a large room, library, or in several adjoining workshop rooms.

The workshop leader is also a key person in successful planning sessions and must be able to provide a relaxed and congenial atmosphere, as well as to give help to individual teams. Familiarity with career education's goals and experience in working with groups of teachers is essential for this individual. Thinking can be stimulated in the atmosphere he creates, and workshops conducted along these lines can be productive, interesting, and exciting. Once workshop teams have worked together a few times, a workshop leader is no longer needed. A pattern of task-oriented objectives has been established which will be carried out by the teachers in their own way.

Paraprofessionals can also be enthusiastic members of the school career education team. They can make community contacts, arrange for equipment, and take groups of students on mini field trips. These paraprofessionals need to be chosen from a different set of criteria from that of teacher aides. They need to be flexible, enthusiastic, fond of young people, and perhaps be in a plateau period of career development themselves. Chronological age has little to do with the criteria. They should have had varied experiences in the world of work. Ex-waitresses, engineers, accountants, and ministers have been found to be successful.

Not all school districts can afford paraprofessionals. Parents who are willing to serve for a specific number of hours a week, counseling interns, junior college and interested high school students often will volunteer time for this purpose. These students, in addition to receiving credit, learn job skills of interviewing, telephone etiquette, working with children, writing reports, using equipment, writing objectives, etc.

When the in-service time is longer, other meaningful experiences can be initiated. For instance, members of the team can spend afternoons on job sites with tape recorders and self-developing cameras and can report back to the group on the following morning; groups can design a line production product and actually produce the product at the workshop site. A five-week workshop in Washington State required each participant to:

(1) Conduct a job interview with someone on the job

(2) Analyze the job into major and minor tasks, personal qualities of the worker, salary range, training necessary, skills required on the job, and outlook for the future

(3) Take a series of slides depicting the job

(4) Write a script from the job interview that would put across the main aspects of the job

(5) Record the script on tape synchronized with slides

The slide-tape packages were prepared for student viewing and were made available to teachers throughout the area. Examples could be expanded interminably. The main points are these:

(1) Career education examples useful for curriculum purposes and covering all of the components of career education can be found everywhere, either by searching out examples to fit a concept or by recognizing the conceptual value of a chance encounter.

(2) Only those career education additions to the curriculum to which the teacher has contributed will have meaning and be used.

(3) Teachers will not be able to develop and use such curricula unless:

(a) They understand the objectives and content of career education.

(b) They have been trained to recognize opportunities and turn them into curricula.

(c) They have time for the exposure to the work world and to plan and prepare materials.

(d) Preparation time, in concert with colleagues, is structured into their working schedule.

All of the foregoing support a formal in-service teacher training and career education planning program for every school district which has serious ambitions for achieving career education goals.

Summary

The intent of this chapter has been to give illustrations of both educator training and in-service training. The major emphasis has obviously been on the in-service training of working teachers, administrators, and counselors. The implication is that as schools begin to change and demand different kinds of personnel, the training institutions will and must respond to these changes. It follows that if the public relations of good programs are as successful as the programs themselves, responsive educator training institutions will become involved by using career education schools as intern locations and by asking career education practitioners to teach courses in the training institutions. Concerned educators can hasten this logical alliance by contacting the teacher training institutions and working out an arrangement whereby academic credit can be given for in-service workshop time. It is then but a short and rewarding step to the recognition by teacher education institutions that such in-service experiences can be incorporated within a preservice sequence.

Suggestions for Further Reading

Association for Student Teaching. *A Guide to Professional Excellence in Clinical Experiences in Teacher Education.* Washington, D.C., 1970.

English, F. W. *Strategies for Differentiated Staffing.* Berkeley, California: McCutchen Publishing Company, 1972.

Etzioni, Anatole. "Human Beings Are Not so Easy to Change After All." *Saturday Review* (April 3, 1972).

Giles, F. T. *Changing Teacher Education in a Large Urban University.* Washington, D.C.: A.A.C.T.E., 1972.

Guba, Egen G. "Methodological Strategies for Educational Change." Paper presented to the Conference on Strategies for Educational Change, Washington, D.C., November 8 to 10, 1965.

Mietus, Walter S. "Industrial Arts Teacher Education in the Age of Institutional Obsolesence." Paper presented to the American Industrial Arts Association's 33d Annual Convention, Miami, Florida, April 22, 1971.

Norton, Robert E., Consulting Editor. "Staff Development Guidelines for Comprehensive Career Education." Columbus, Ohio: Center for Vocational and Technical Education, Ohio State University, May 1972.

Pataline, Marianne. *Rationale and Use of Content-Relevant Achievement Tests for the Evaluation of Instructional Programs.* Report no. 56. Los Angeles, California: Center for the Study of Evaluation, University of California, May 1970.

Shaffer, Warren F.; and Hughes, Donald E. "A Research-Based Interview: Its Effect on Teachers' Classroom Behavior." *Elementary School Guidance and Counseling Journal* 6:4 (May 1972).

Sower, Christopher. *The Normative Sponsorship Theory of Updating Organizations.* East Lansing, Michigan: Michigan State University, 1968.

Tyler, Ralph W., Editor. "Educational Evaluations: New Roles, New Means." *Sixty-eighth Yearbook, Part II.* The National Society for the Study of Education. Chicago: University of Chicago Press, 1969.

7

Strategy
and
Reward

These chapters have provided a rationale for career education in the elementary school, offered examples from scattered school experience, and suggested both technique and content for program implementation. The book has addressed elementary school teachers as its primary audience, and if it has been persuasive, change should occur in at least a few classrooms and school communities.

No major lasting change can or should occur in American education without the active support and involvement of the classroom teacher. The edicts of the school administrator, the rhetoric of the educational philosopher, the findings of the educational researcher, and the voice of the general public can all be effectively ignored by the teacher through simply closing the classroom door and facing the students. Career education can never happen unless teachers are convinced of its worth and viability. At the same time, elementary school teachers rarely have total discretion in their classroom activities and never have full control over the resources required. The education machine is huge with tremendous inertia; that is, it has tremendous energy in its direction of motion. Teachers must perceive career education as rewarding to them and must contribute to strategies for its endorsement by educational administrators, public opinion makers, and the community. This chapter attempts to answer questions about career education often asked by elementary school teachers, and suggests strategies for extending endorsements of the concept.

TEACHER CONCERNS ABOUT CAREER EDUCATION

Teacher endorsement of career education depends upon the extent to which it corresponds to teachers' perceptions of student welfare and their own professional identities. Teacher resistance will be directly related to the extent to which teachers themselves are asked to change their attitudes, their philosophies, their competencies, and their teaching methodologies, without conviction that these changes are needed. Since career education asks teachers to change in all of these ways, it is extremely vulnerable to teacher reaction. Some advocates of career education have assigned to classroom teachers a greater share of the blame for current shortcomings than they deserve, and a greater portion of the responsibility for change than they can possibly assume on their own. Thus it is not surprising that large numbers of highly competent, conscientious, professional teachers have unresolvable doubts regarding their role in career education and the viability of the concept itself.

Many teacher questions pertain to such routine administrative matters as how they are to be given the time required to adapt their lesson plans to the career education concept, how they are to acquire the knowledge and experience required for their participation in career education, and how and where they can obtain career education materials for use in the classroom. Those questions that cost money are the easiest to answer. If both school administrators and the general public are convinced of a concept's importance, they will provide the money as rapidly as possible. The hard questions are those related to the teacher's professional commitment to the concept. It is those answers which will determine how much the teacher is willing to give of himself or herself in converting the concept into reality. Since some of those questions will be in the minds of the readers of this book, discussion of some of these frequently raised issues may be useful.[1]

• *What is this career education I keep hearing about? Everybody talks about it but nobody tells me how to do it. The statements I read*

---

[1] Adapted from Kenneth B. Hoyt, *Guidance Newsletter* (Service Research Associates, 1972–73), no. 3.

about it are often contradictory. It is hoped that this volume will have conributed to alleviating the how to do it concern. Concepts of career education differ widely among its advocates. For some, it is vocational education in a new guise; for others, it encompasses all education. For some, it is for the noncollege-bound; and for still others, it encompasses college, adult learning, industrial training, and all of the formal and informal learnings concerning productive activity throughout a lifetime.

If the conception is too narrow, it will change little; if too broad, it becomes devoid of meaning. The current outpouring of writings about career education will undoubtedly lead eventually to a more coherent synthesis. At the same time, the teacher should never expect a blueprint. The career education which fits the teacher and the class will be that curriculum which emerges from the teacher's perceptions and efforts to give reality to the concepts.

- *U.S. Office of Education priorities come and go with the political winds. Why should I revise my whole teaching approach only to see career education superseded shortly by a new panacea?* If career education were really new and only an Office of Education invention, one would be wise to adopt a "wait and see" attitude before making a major investment of time and effort. However, what is currently called career education is only a modest extension, though a general endorsement, of trends which have been under way for at least a decade. It has grown out of concern for the demonstrated difficulty American youth experience in making the transition from the world of school to the world of work. It is a culmination of more than ten years of conceptualization, research, and experiment.

Knowledge of these experiments has not been widespread, and therein lies the greatest contribution of the Office of Education — aggressive endorsement and dissemination of the concept. The nation will remain concerned with increased output from its expanding investment in education, it will insist that young people enter the adult world with productive values and skills, and it will reject the inegalitarian emphasis upon college education as the only really acceptable preparation for life. These and other incentives for adoption of something like career education will remain, regardless of federal education priorities.

- *My classroom day is already crowded with subject matter and skills which must be taught. What shall I throw out if I must bring career education into the classroom as well?* Throw out nothing. Teachers have been deluged with instructions to include concepts of environmental education, drug education, sex education, citizenship education, etc., and know these cannot all be accomplished in the time available. If career education represents an addition to this list of subject matter to be covered, the concept has not been clarified. The point must be once again emphasized. Career education is at once an objective and a method for all education. Using career interest as a vehicle and a motivator for knowledge already purveyed and tapping learning resources outside the classroom must increase the productivity of instructional hours *or it should not be undertaken.*

There will be many times when a discussion of career implications is simply not appropriate, and if inserted would be distracting and wasteful of time. The use of career relevance as a form of educational motivation is best judged by the teacher. One career education objective is to provide teachers with another means of helping students see that school can make sense for them. It is designed to help students learn more, not less, of the substantive content the teacher is trying to get across to students. If this is done correctly, students should be better prepared for further education, as well as for work, than if this form of educational motivation were to go unused. The assumption is that if students are made aware of the career implications of their subjects, increases in student learning will take place. This assumption has already been tested and verified in many classrooms with various groups of students. It is certainly one that could be easily tested in any school.

• *My teaching goals are much broader than simply preparing students to work. How can I teach career implications without detracting from other worthy educational objectives?* Many teachers are disturbed by statements of one or two advocates of career education that all education should be career education. They are reminded of past pronouncements that all education is progressive education. All education should *not* be concentrated around the goals of career education. Preparation for making a living is only one of a number of worthy goals of American education. Much of the work today's students can look forward to doing will carry no economic rewards whatsoever.

Preparation for making a living is only part of preparation for living itself. There is nothing new about the contention that American education should be concerned about helping students learn how to make a living. This has been one of the stated goals of American education in every major policy statement on education that has been promulgated during the 20th century. The trouble is, it has been the one goal that has never been successfully implemented in educational practice for all of the children of all of the people. The "school for schooling's sake" emphasis has made education seem to be an end in itself. Whatever education is, it certainly must be viewed as preparation for *something* — preparation for making a living, preparation for enjoying life, preparation for good citizenship, preparation for home and family living, preparation for intellectual activity . . . but preparation for something.

Career education merely avers that education as preparation for making a living has not received as much emphasis as it deserves. With the increasingly close relationships now existing between education and work, it is an educational purpose that can no longer be ignored.

• *With the current uncertainty regarding the future nature of occupations, the dehumanizing nature of some work, and the probability of continuing high youth unemployment, is career education's emphasis on education as preparation for work a wise direction for American education to take?* Some find it anachronistic that education should raise the priority of employability and productivity among its objectives just when, as they perceive it, work is of declining importance in the economy and in life. They misread the signals. Leisure has increased slowly as the fruits of productivity have been divided between higher incomes and more time off the job. But the threat is that productivity will decline, not accelerate. Much of the rising productivity which allowed the choice between income and leisure was a product of the transfer from low-productivity agriculture to high-productivity manufacturing. The transfer of labor to service industries has the opposite effect. The four-day week is a repackaging of the standard forty hours, not a decrease of work time. Increased time spent in transportation to and from work rarely has leisure value.

The nature of work and the work ethic is changing. Much of what was once done by hand is now done by machine. It is also true that many additional things now done by human labor could also be automated, were it not that people are willing to do these tasks more cheaply than machines. Nevertheless, it remains true that economically speaking, "there ain't no free lunch." Individual incomes and national strength still rest upon productivity. Some can live without work only by lowering the standard of living of all. We are wealthy enough as a society to afford to support those who cannot work for a variety of reasons. We also have the wealth to support many who contribute in ways not measured by wages and salaries in the labor market. Still it also remains true that no society can survive without work. Moreover, he who does not contribute in some way to society's well-being soon feels himself a parasite, even if his culture does not condemn him. If the school prepares people for life, it must prepare them for work and for some type of personally defined work ethic within which they can respect themselves. One can argue about the *nature* of work, but there can be no argument about its *necessity*. Preparation for work is, in a democratic society, simply part of preparation for good citizenship.

The current concern with the demeaning and dehumanizing nature of some jobs is justified, but such jobs represent a limited and declining margin of the job world. It is the repetitive assembly-line job which is most easily "automated." The trends, with more and more workers producing services and more and more machines producing good products, are in the direction of humanizing, not dehumanizing work and workers. As more and more of the work that people do demand specific job skills requiring educational preparation, the movement is toward a relatively greater degree of autonomy *and thus of humanness* because the degree of direction the worker can exert in the performance of his job duties is decreasing. The trends point to an emphasis on making work more meaningful and more satisfying to the individual worker. A career education emphasis can make positive contributions toward helping workers themselves speed up this process.

The fact that the rapidity of occupational change will force many people to make numerous occupational choices during their lifetimes is related to how people *implement* their work values, but not to the degree to which they *hold* and cherish such values for themselves. True, our occupational society is changing at a rapid rate requiring greater adaptability on the part of all individuals. Nevertheless, at any point in time, the occupational society does have a structure, and new entrants must view it as it exists. If our schools would worry more about helping students take the next step after they leave school and avoid a posture that says, "We must do nothing until we know exactly what the future holds," they would serve youth better.

The primary reason that youth suffers more unemployment now than in the past is that there are so many more of them. But some portion is undoubtedly due to the fact that they have not equipped themselves with the kinds of occupational skills that society now needs, nor with the kinds of work values that will lead them to see work as a meaningful and satisfying part of their lives. The current high rate of youth unemployment represents a basic *reason* for installing the career education concept, not an excuse for *resisting* it.

The Elementary School Role in Career Education

Where does the elementary school fit in career education's assignment to make work *possible, meaningful,* and *satisfying* to each individual? The kindergarten through sixth grade student is a long way from labor market entry, yet is developing attitudes which may determine later career success or failure. The elementary school can help make work possible by motivating the student (1) to think about himself as a prospective worker and (2) to recognize the importance of mastering subject matter content through demonstration of the career implications of that subject matter, and to acquire good work habits. It should not be forgotten that the ability to apply one's self to a classroom task is not essentially different from the ability to apply one's self in a work setting as employee or manager.

Work can be made more meaningful to elementary school students by teaching about the basic value of work, the environments within which it occurs, the contributions that work makes to society, and about work values. The school can help make work satisfying to students by giving them credit for the use of good work habits, by creating situations where they can see positive accomplishments resulting from the work they do, and by creating a reward system associated with that work. With rare exceptions, none of this is part of the current elementary school curriculum.

During the time that a child is in the elementary school is none too early to teach decision-making skills, but it is not the time to encourage even tentative career choices. Labor market entrance is too many years away, and the occupational society continues to change. The child is still in a fantasy stage of career development. Each child will probably express frequent and changing occupational preferences, but there is nothing to gain and much to lose by encouraging the student to think of any of those choices as reasoned or permanent. Differential aptitudes do not begin to be apparent (or we do not know how to recognize or measure them) until beyond elementary school.

Even educational choices — whether or not to go to college, etc. — are too far away for serious consideration at this point. In fact, encouraging students to think in such terms will lead them to cut off major portions of the occupational world, without opportunity to consider and reconsider them in realistic terms later.

Thus to concentrate on attitude development, the development of work habits and realization of the career implications of academic subject matter will give the elementary school a major piece of the career education action, without foreclosing decisions which are best made in later life.

Winning Community Acceptance

Widespread adoption of career education concepts and practices in the elementary school will require more than teacher advocacy, though that may well be the single most vital factor in its durability. It *will* require whole-hearted and immediate community support. The children, who stand to gain the most, are the most responsive and also the most powerless. Parents, who stand to gain next, are suspicious of educational change, especially if the result is pedagogy different from that which they remember . . . any apparent loosening of discipline and any hint that "my child" will not be carried or driven to occupational heights beyond parental attainment. For them, the message must *not* be "Your child need not go to college," a message that may be misleading as well as distasteful. The true career education promise is that whatever educational level is attained, the full opportunity to learn the prerequisite attitudes, knowledge, and skills for occupational success will have been provided by the community.

Employers should grasp career education's promise quickly and enthusiastically if the message is accurately and honestly relayed. The labor organizations will applaud if they are provided a role. The legislator and school board will ask what it will cost and what it will offer. The school administrator is most likely to respond cautiously until convinced. The new emphasis means a greater strain on his personal resources and the administrative adjustments of reorientation and reform.

Teacher education institutions will likely be the most reluctant. University faculties die more often than they change, but a buyers' market for elementary teachers should bypass those who do not conform to consumer requirements. Educational associations will react from the vested interests of their particular membership. The career education advocate must pursue support with whatever strategy and leverage is at hand.

No one should suggest that career education will be without cost, even in the elementary school, though assurance of increased cost effectiveness can be given. The retraining of teachers and the preparation of new materials will all require expenditures. Teachers cannot teach what they do not know, and thus will need compensation for summers and other nonteaching time spent familiarizing themselves with the work world outside the school, and preparing curriculum materials. Industry may require some compensation for the costs of its cooperation. However, once career education is in place, there should be only two characteristics which should lead to higher costs than present practices. One is the possibility of employer compensation for interference with production. The other and more certain one is the necessity of greater individualization of instruction, already needed but now more readily ignored.

On the other hand, many potential costs will be offset by the free services available from parents, employers, public agencies, labor organizations, and retired and cooperating workers. Getting out of the classroom should not be much more expensive than remaining in it, and most of those who visit the classroom will provide voluntary service. The outlook is for substantial initial costs followed by slightly higher operating costs, which will be offset by a significantly improved product.

But what evidence is there that career education will make a difference? Society seems convinced that it has paid for a junkyard of educational reforms which appear to have made little added contribution. Despite this logic, all advocates should admit the limited history of the evidences for career education, particularly in the elementary school. All that can be promised is careful evaluation of an effort which at least has more measurable objectives. Final evaluation of career education can follow only after a generation has experienced it and tried the careers which follow it, through an educational and working lifetime. Interim tests can be found in the promise that career education can enhance the learning of academic subjects. That is a testable claim with short-time horizons and adaptable to control group comparisons. Preliminary applications of this test are already available with favorable results. Many more tests should follow; not only of whether, but for whom and under what conditions can career relevance aid academic learning.

The objective knowledge of occupations and labor market realities gained by children are testable, as are their attitudes toward occupations and work. How this knowledge and attitude affect subsequent careers is again a generation-long assessment.

After students have left the formal school, dropout, placement, job retention, and job progress rates are all measurable and comparable to control groups. Such evaluations should be designed and built into career education methodology to produce the needed authentication or the deserved rejection, whatever the case may be, as early as possible. The career education program in the elementary schools, however, will need to be measured in terms of increased degree of student success in further career education, in advanced academic education, and in increased student satisfaction. Meanwhile, the logic and the dissatisfaction with current methods and results should be sufficient justification for widespread implementation and trial.

At present, career education appears to have no concerted opponents, though there are those who resist change, those who fear that career education will be used to discriminate against minorities, and those who fear reallocation of resources in which they have vested interests. The greatest resistance is likely to come from those simply made cynical by past failures of vaunted reform with high price tags.

The pressing need is for initiatives to move ahead into a largely unresisting vacuum. Whoever will take the initiative can share the credit for the progress. Legislators can reshape laws which pose obstacles to career education. School boards can reallocate resources and redirect policy. School administrators have the power to inaugurate new programs and develop and initiate new techniques. Teachers have the ultimate power to do their own thing, at least to some degree, in the classroom. Employers and labor organizations can offer assistance, and parents and taxpayers can demand change. In other words, there is no general strategy we can prescribe. Each individual or community must start from its present position, and using the authority and persuasion at hand, proceed to where it wants to go.

The ultimate goal and reward are not only a reduction in the social distance between the top and the bottom of our occupational hierarchy, it is the enormous potential of a generation who are experienced in planning and who are resourceful and have self-control. For the elementary school, the vision may be more concrete.

Because of lower birth rates, elementary school enrollments will fall by two million by 1980, freeing finances, teachers, and faculties. Consequently, the added costs may not be noticeable. Teachers may need special skills to protect them in their jobs. Space and time may be available — given simultaneous trends of earlier retirement, increased leisure, and interest in adult education — for generations to learn together. The elementary school teacher, rather than serving as a baby-sitter for 35 children, may become the orchestrator of community resources and learning environments. Children may learn to value work later on in life, but will recognize the joys of service now.

One reward is readily apparent in those schools and among those elementary school teachers who have already endorsed and implemented career education: an increased enthusiasm for the role of teacher — "I never knew that teaching could be such fun" . . . "It gets us out of the assembly-line education concept of the first grade as preparation for the second grade and gives us specific objectives related to life rather than more school." These archetypal comments — capped by the ultimate in commitment: "If our experimental grant is not renewed next year, we will go on pursuing career education with our own resources" and "We've never had such support from the community. They wouldn't let us stop if we wanted to" — are heard on every front. One implication may be more autonomy for the teacher, in a profession increasingly constrained by many of the aspects of an assembly line. If the objective of career education — to make work possible, meaningful, and satisfying to each individual — is good for the kids, why should it not be equally good for the teachers?

Though much of the foregoing is yet in the "maybe" stage, we can be sure of several things:

(1) Education is increasingly in disrepute and must be refurbished with more demonstrable performance.

(2) Dissatisfaction is present in the world of work. Although it is disquieting for us to hear and see this dissatisfaction, we must recognize that it indeed exists and that somewhere, someone must help to restore the work ethic to dignity.

(3) Career education may be the *only* available approach to a simultaneous solution to these two social challenges. So why not use it?

Suggestions for Further Reading

Instructor Magazine, The. February 1972.

Olympus Research Corporation. *Career Education: A Handbook for Implementation.* Washington, D.C.: U.S. Government Printing Office, 1972.

——————. *Career Education in the Environment: A Handbook for Implementation.* Washington, D.C.: U.S. Government Printing Office, 1972.

Portola Institute. *The Last Whole Earth Catalog.* Menlo Park, California: Random House.

Wurman, Richard. "The Yellow Pages of Learning Resources." Boston: Massachusetts Institute of Technology, 1972.

Index

DATE DUE

MR 07 '86	MAR 27 '86		
GAYLORD			PRINTED IN U.S.A